P9-CCS-018

991 9100 376 137 6

Writing the Critical Essay

ENDANGERED SPECIES

An **OPPOSING**  **VIEWPOINTS®** Guide

Lauri S. Friedman, *Book Editor*

Christine Nasso, *Publisher*
Elizabeth Des Chenes, *Managing Editor*

**OPPOSING
VIEWPOINTS®
SERIES**

GREENHAVEN PRESS
A part of Gale, Cengage Learning

 GALE
CENGAGE Learning·

Detroit • New York • San Francisco • New Haven, Conn • Waterville, Maine • London

© 2008 Gale, a part of Cengage Learning

For more information, contact
Greenhaven Press
27500 Drake Rd.
Farmington Hills, MI 48331-3535
Or you can visit our Internet site at gale.cengage.com

ALL RIGHTS RESERVED.
No part of this work covered by the copyright herein may be reproduced or used in any form or by any means—graphic, electronic, or mechanical, including photocopying, recording, taping, Web distribution, or information storage retrieval systems—without the written permission of the publisher.

Articles in Greenhaven Press anthologies are often edited for length to meet page requirements. In addition, original titles of these works are changed to clearly present the main thesis and to explicitly indicate the author's opinion. Every effort is made to ensure that Greenhaven Press accurately reflects the original intent of the authors. Every effort has been made to trace the owners of copyrighted material.

LIBRARY OF CONGRESS CATALOGING-IN-PUBLICATION DATA

Endangered species / Lauri S. Friedman, book editor.
   p. cm. — (Writing the critical essay)
  Includes bibliographical references and index.
  ISBN-13: 978-0-7377-3856-8 (hardcover)
  1. Endangered species—Juvenile literature. I. Friedman, Lauri S.
  QL83.E546 2007
  333.95'22—dc22

                    2007030798

ISBN-10: 0-7377-3856-1 (hardcover)

Printed in the United States of America
2 3 4 5 6 7 12 11 10 09 08

CONTENTS

Examining the state of writing and how it is taught in the United States was the official purpose of the National Commission on Writing in America's Schools and Colleges. The commission, made up of teachers, school administrators, business leaders, and college and university presidents, released its first report in 2003. "Despite the best efforts of many educators," commissioners argued, "writing has not received the full attention it deserves." Among the findings of the commission was that most fourth-grade students spent less than three hours a week writing, that three-quarters of high school seniors never receive a writing assignment in their history or social studies classes, and that more than 50 percent of first-year students in college have problems writing error-free papers. The commission called for a "cultural sea change" that would increase the emphasis on writing for both elementary and secondary schools. These conclusions have made some educators realize that writing must be emphasized in the curriculum. As colleges are demanding an ever-higher level of writing proficiency from incoming students, schools must respond by making students more competent writers. In response to these concerns, the SAT, an influential standardized test used for college admissions, required an essay for the first time in 2005.

Books in the Writing the Critical Essay: An Opposing Viewpoints Guide series use the patented Opposing Viewpoints format to help students learn to organize ideas and arguments and to write essays using common critical writing techniques. Each book in the series focuses on a particular type of essay writing—including expository, persuasive, descriptive, and narrative—that students learn while being taught both the five-paragraph essay as well as longer pieces of writing that have an opinionated focus. These guides include everything necessary to help students research, outline, draft, edit, and ultimately write successful essays across the curriculum, including essays for the SAT.

Using Opposing Viewpoints

This series is inspired by and builds upon Greenhaven Press's acclaimed Opposing Viewpoints series. As in the parent series, each book in the Writing the Critical Essay series focuses on a timely and controversial social issue that provides lots of opportunities for creating thought-provoking essays. The first section of each volume begins with a brief introductory essay that provides context for the opposing viewpoints that follow. These articles are chosen for their accessibility and clearly stated views. The thesis of each article is made explicit in the article's title and is accentuated by its pairing with an opposing or alternative view. These essays are both models of persuasive writing techniques and valuable research material that students can mine to write their own informed essays. Guided reading and discussion questions help lead students to key ideas and writing techniques presented in the selections.

The second section of each book begins with a preface discussing the format of the essays and examining characteristics of the featured essay type. Model five-paragraph and longer essays then demonstrate that essay type. The essays are annotated so that key writing elements and techniques are pointed out to the student. Sequential, step-by-step exercises help students construct and refine thesis statements; organize material into outlines; analyze and try out writing techniques; write transitions, introductions, and conclusions; and incorporate quotations and other researched material. Ultimately, students construct their own compositions using the designated essay type.

The third section of each volume provides additional research material and writing prompts to help the student. Additional facts about the topic of the book serve as a convenient source of supporting material for essays. Other features help students go beyond the book for their research. Like other Greenhaven Press books, each book in the Writing the Critical Essay series includes bibliographic listings of relevant periodical articles, books, Web sites, and organizations to contact.

Writing the Critical Essay: An Opposing Viewpoints Guide will help students master essay techniques that can be used in any discipline.

The Environment and the Economy: A Symbiotic Relationship

The interests of the economy and the interests of the environment are often pitted against each other as if they were polar opposites. Yet in truth, this is rarely the case. On a very basic level, humans need a healthy environment to survive and flourish. They depend on ecosystems such as oceans, estuaries, grasslands, wetlands, forests, and plains to supply them with clean air, water, and abundant food. They need the environment to be healthy enough so that its many resources—such as animals used for food, plants used for medicine, and raw materials used for building—can be used to improve human lives. In this way, plant and animal species form the foundation of not only healthy ecosystems but healthy economies. Therefore, humans have a vested interest in protecting endangered species for their own survival and well-being.

A healthy and sustained environment is often critical to preserving business interests that depend upon environmental plenty. Nick Dusic, science policy analyst for the British Ecological Society, explains why caring for the environment is critical to our own survival: "The services that ecosystems provide are fundamental to our well-being. . . . When we over-exploit fish stocks, our economy grows more slowly than it otherwise would, due to the loss of the fishing industry. When we log upland forests, we are less secure due to the increased risk of flooding. When we pollute freshwater ecosystems, we are less healthy due to poor water quality."[1]

[1] Nick Dusic, "Secure People Need Healthy Ecosystems," British Ecological Society, September 2005. www.the-ba.net/the-BA/CurrentIssues/ReportsandPublications/ ScienceAndPublicAffairs/SPASept05/Ecosystems.htm

Actress Betty White (left) and anthropologist Jane Goodall (right) come together at a news conference to discuss the environment and endangered species issues facing the United States.

One example of how the loss of species can negatively affect the economy is found in the mass over-fishing currently going on around the planet. In 2005, a disturbing study published in the journal *Science* predicted that humans would completely over-fish wild seafood stocks by the year 2050. Stanford University scientist Steve Palumbi, one of the scientists on the project, said of the findings: "Unless we fundamentally change the way we manage all the ocean species together, as working ecosystems, then this century is the last century of wild seafood."[2] The worldwide fishing industry employs millions of people and contributes to multi-billions of dollars each year. If there were no more wild seafood to commercially fish, the lack of industry could trigger an economic crisis that would ripple around the globe.

Another example of how economic interests are dependant upon a healthy environment is found closer to home, in the Pacific Northwest region of the United States. Here, various species of fish, such as salmon, are commercially raised, directly benefiting local economies. The National Wildlife Federation's Endangered Species Program estimates that commercial salmon fishing in the region provides 60,000 jobs and $1 billion annually in revenues. This industry and regional way of life, however, is threatened as salmon decline due to habitat degradation from dams, clearing of forests, and overgrazing along streams. If the salmon's habitat is not properly protected it has grave consequences, not just for the fish, but for the economic health of the local community that thrives off of them. During a 1999 effort in Washington to preserve salmon habitat, Seattle's mayor, Paul Schell, noted the connection between the health of local salmon and the health of local industry, saying, "As we work to save the salmon, it may turn out that the salmon save us."[3]

Freshwater mussels are another species that support a local economy. The harvesting of the mussels in various bodies of water supports approximately 100,000 American jobs and contributes more than $700 million to the economy each year. But it is estimated that about 43 percent of the different freshwater mussel species in North America are currently endangered or extinct. If the species declines any further, many Americans will lose their livelihoods.

Preserving endangered species and their habitat has yet another economic value: tourism dollars. Indeed, many plant and animal species and their ecosystems form the basis

---

2 Quoted in Richard Black, "'Only 50 Years Left' for Sea Fish," November 2, 2006. BBC News. http://news.bbc.co.uk/2/hi/science/nature/6108414.stm
3 "Saving a Regional Icon," *New York Times*, March 18 1999.

of America's multi-billion dollar, employment-rich tourism industry. It is estimated that every year in the U.S., approximately 110 million people participate in wildlife-related recreation, such as bird-watching, hiking, biking, boating, photography, and many other activities. Americans spend over $59 billion annually on travel, lodging, equipment, and food to engage in wildlife recreation. In New Jersey alone, nearly 14.2 million visits are made to regional wilderness areas each year, bringing in about $304 million in revenue and supporting 7,000 jobs. For these reasons, the authors of a report on the economic value of New Jersey's wild areas write, "The State parks and forests represent economically productive 'assets' which are in many cases irreplaceable. Their preservation and enhancement therefore makes good economic sense and good public policy."[4]

All of these are examples of the fact that when humans endanger species, they do so at their own peril. As the environment, and environmentally-based economies, continue to suffer, it becomes increasingly clear that everyone has some interest in environmental protection, just as everyone has some interest in the preservation of business and economic well-being. As author John Roush puts it, "No one—not even the most dedicated environmentalist—wants to go without food, shelter, and a livelihood," and "no one—not even the most dedicated industrialist or miner—wants to go without clean air and water and green places."[5] For these reasons conservation efforts should be applauded by everyone, especially those who make their living from natural resources.

Balancing the needs of the environment with the needs of the economy is a tricky enterprise, yet one that is important to master. How far society should go to protect endangered

[4] William J. Mates and Jorge L. Reyes, "The Economic Value of New Jersey State Parks and Forests," New Jersey Department of Environmental Protection, Division of Science, Research & Technology. June 2004. http://www.state.nj.us/dep/dsr/economics/parksforest-report.pdf
[5] John Roush, "The Biggest Threat to Wilderness" International Journal of Wilderness, Vol. 1, No. 1, September 1995.

species is a continuing source of debate, and one that is likely to become a more frequent fixture of both environmental and economic discussion of the 21st century. *Writing the Critical Essay: An Opposing Viewpoints Guide: Endangered Species* exposes readers to the basic arguments made about endangered species and helps them develop tools to craft their own essays on the subject.

The United States takes an active role in dealing with the issues and concerns of endangered species.

Section One: Opposing Viewpoints on Endangered Species

Species Extinction Is a Serious Problem

World Conservation Union

In the following viewpoint, the World Conservation Union argues that the problem of species extinction is serious and getting worse. Though species extinction is a natural and gradual process, the authors present evidence that shows that humans have caused species to become extinct at a rate 100 to 11,000 times greater than natural extinction rates. Human activities such as pollution, building, and development that has caused habitat loss, and overhunting and overfishing have caused the increasing extinction and endangerment of mammals, fish, birds, reptiles, and plants, write the authors. They urge humanity to undertake efforts on individual and global scales to prevent species and habitat loss.

The World Conservation Union is the world's largest conservation network, bringing together 82 states, 111 government agencies, more than 800 non-governmental organizations (NGOs), and some 10,000 scientists and experts from 181 countries to influence, encourage and assist societies throughout the world to conserve the integrity and diversity of nature.

The World Conservation Union, "Species Extinction: A Natural—and Unnatural—Process," The World Conservation Union, 2004. Copyright © 1995-2006 International Union for Conservation of Nature and Natural Resources. All rights reserved. Reproduced by permission.

Consider the Following Questions:

1. What is the meaning of "the sixth extinction crisis," as explained by the authors?
2. According to the authors, at least how many extinctions have occurred since 1500?
3. What four countries have the most threatened mammals and birds, as reported by the authors?

The world is, and always has been, in a state of flux. Even the land beneath our feet is constantly on the move. Over hundreds of millions of years, continents have broken apart, oceans appeared, mountains formed and worn inexorably away.

These processes continue, barely discernible over a single human life-time. With geological change come changes in living things: species, populations, and whole lineages disappear, and new ones emerge.

The entire basis of organic evolution is underpinned by the appearance of some species and the disappearance of others; extinction is therefore a natural process.

According to the fossil record, no species has yet proved immortal; as few as 2-4% of the species that have ever lived are believed to survive today. The remainder are extinct, the vast majority having disappeared long before the arrival of humans.

Extinctions and Humans

Extinctions caused by humans are generally considered to be a recent, modern phenomenon. However, humanity's first significant contribution to the rate of global extinction may have occurred during the past 100,000 years, when North and South America and Australia lost 74 to 86% of the genera of "megafauna"—mammals greater than 44 kg.

In Australia, where the earliest human remains are dated to approximately 64,000 years, the great majority of the 22 identified genera of large land animals disappeared between 30,000 and 60,000 years ago.

In the Americas, almost 80% of large-bodied genera became extinct. Extraordinary creatures, such as sabre-toothed cats, mammoths, giant armoured glyptodonts and giant ground-sloths, all disappeared some time between 11,000 and 13,000 years ago, coinciding with the dates of the first clear evidence of a human presence there.

Island megafaunas—like giant birds known as moas in New Zealand, the dodo on Mauritius, giant lemurs and the extraordinary elephant bird in Madagascar, or large rodents and ground-sloths in the Caribbean—survived until much more recently than the continental faunas. All seem to have disappeared within a few hundred years after the arrival of humans—in the case of the moas within the last 300 years.

The "Sixth Wave"

The rapid loss of species that we are witnessing today is estimated by some experts to be between 100 and 1,000 times higher than the "background" or expected natural extinction rate (this is a highly conservative estimate: some studies estimate current extinction rates as 1,000–11,000 times background rates). Unlike the mass-extinction events of geological history, the current extinction phenomenon is one for which a single species—ours—appears to be almost wholly responsible. Such a deteriorating situation is being referred to as "the sixth extinction crisis", after the five known extinction waves in the Ordovican, Devonian, Permian, Triassic and Cretaceous Periods.

Saving Species to Save Ourselves

The services that ecosystems provide are fundamental to our well-being. . . .When we over-exploit fish stocks, our economy grows more slowly than it otherwise would, due to the loss of the fishing industry. When we log upland forests, we are less secure due to the increased risk of flooding. When we pollute freshwater ecosystems, we are less healthy due to poor water quality.

Nick Dusic, "Secure People Need Healthy Ecosystems," British Ecological Society, September 2005.

The frequently asked question of "how many species have gone extinct in the last 100 years" is difficult to answer because of problems in recording contemporary extinction events. Decline and eventual extinction may take place over many years, or even centuries in the case of very long-lived organisms like some of the large mammal and tree species.

The final stages of extinction are seldom observed except those caused by extreme events such as the excessive hunting of the passenger pigeon (*Ectopistes migratorius*) or the mass extinction of native snails in French Polynesia and Hawaii following the introduction of the predatory snail (*Euglandina rosea*) to Pacific Islands. Since 1500 AD, 844 extinctions have been recorded.

The Extinction Problem Is Worse Than Feared

The *2004 IUCN Red List of Threatened Species* tells us that the global extinction crisis is as bad, or worse, than we believed.

A total of 15,589 species of plants and animals are known to face a high risk of extinction in the near future, in almost all cases as a result of human activities. This includes 32% (one in three) of amphibian species, 24% (one in four) of mammal species, 12% (one in eight) of bird species, 25% (one in four) of conifers and 52% of cycads (an ancient group of plants).

Indonesia, India, Brazil and China are among the countries with the most threatened mammals and birds, while plant species are declining rapidly in South and Central America, Central and West Africa, and Southeast Asia.

The IUCN Red List highlights the plight of a range of animals and plants, from the Pemba flying fox to the King Pilly pine.

Aders duiker (*Cephalophus adersi*). This antelope, which occurs in Kenya and Tanzania, moved from endangered to critically endangered since 2003 because of substantial population declines caused by declining habitat and illegal hunting.

The state of the world's threatened bird species is worse than ever. Since 1994 the number of bird species threatened with global extinction has risen to 12%. Of the new total,

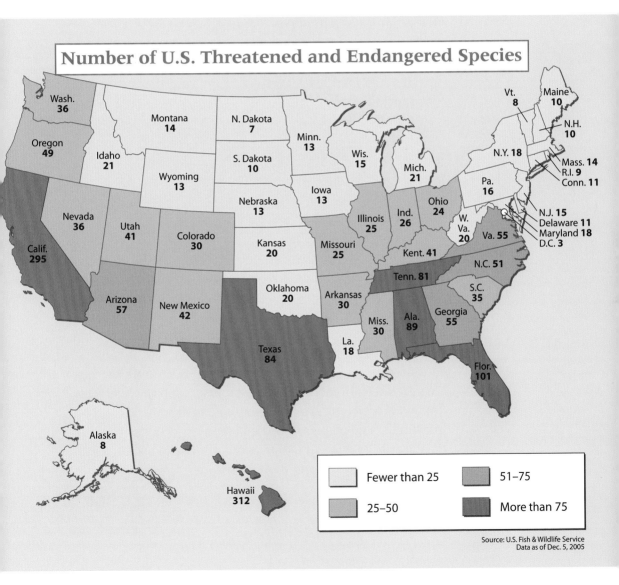

Number of U.S. Threatened and Endangered Species

Wash.	36
Oregon	49
Idaho	21
Montana	14
Wyoming	13
N. Dakota	7
S. Dakota	10
Minn.	13
Wis.	15
Mich.	21
Nevada	36
Utah	41
Colorado	30
Nebraska	13
Iowa	13
Illinois	25
Ind.	26
Ohio	24
Calif.	295
Arizona	57
New Mexico	42
Kansas	20
Missouri	25
Kent.	41
W. Va.	20
Va.	55
Pa.	16
N.Y.	18
Vt.	8
Maine	10
N.H.	10
Mass.	14
R.I.	9
Conn.	11
N.J.	15
Delaware	11
Maryland	18
D.C.	3
Oklahoma	20
Arkansas	30
Tenn.	81
N.C.	51
S.C.	35
Miss.	30
Ala.	89
Georgia	55
La.	18
Texas	84
Flor.	101
Alaska	8
Hawaii	312

Legend:
- Fewer than 25
- 25–50
- 51–75
- More than 75

Source: U.S. Fish & Wildlife Service
Data as of Dec. 5, 2005

1,175 (99%) are at risk of extinction from human activities.

Sao Tome free-tailed bat (*Chaerephon tomensis*). This bat has moved up the threatened scale from vulnerable to critically endangered. It is known to occur in only two sites, despite extensive searches. Its coastal forest and savanna habitats are being destroyed through tourism and agricultural development.

Reptiles and Plants Are Also at Risk

The number of threatened reptiles increased from 253 in 1996 to 304 in 2004. The number of critically endangered species has increased from 41 to 64, and the number of endangered species has increased from 59 to 79 species.

St Helena olive (*Nesiota elliptica*). Listed in 2003 as extinct in the wild, this symbolic species is now extinct. The last known tree surviving in the wild died in 1994 and the only known plant still in cultivation died in November 2003. No other live material (plants, seeds or tissues) remain in local or international collections.

A total of 8,321 threatened plants are listed. This is around 2% of the world's described plants, but as only approximately 4% of the world's described plants have been evaluated, the true percentage of threatened plant species is much higher.

Giant Hispaniolan galliwasp (*Celestus warreni*). Moving from near threatened to critically endangered, this lizard is thought to have declined by at least 80% over the last 20 years. It is threatened by habitat loss, especially deforestation for agricultural activities (planting crops and creating pastures). The galliwasp is also killed by local people who mistakenly consider it to be venomous. Galliwasps are also killed by dogs, cats, and mongooses.

The Major Threats

Almost all the factors that have led to the extinction of species in the modern era continue to operate, many with ever-increasing intensity. While these factors vary in intensity and relative importance in the three major biomes (the land, inland waters and the seas), certain common threads emerge.

The Osprey is a rare bird that faces extinction, and very few are found worldwide today.

Meat from wild animals (wild meat) forms a critical contribution to food sources and livelihoods in many areas particularly in countries with high levels of poverty and food insecurity. A huge range of species are involved including monkeys, tapirs, antelopes, pigs, pheasants, turtles and snakes.

The diversity of nature helps meet the recreational, emotional, cultural, spiritual and aesthetic needs of people.

Can Extinction Be Stopped?

It takes huge efforts at all levels, from individual to global, to halt species extinction, a constant input and analysis of data on species, their habitats and threats.

Analyze the Essay:

1. After reading this viewpoint, do you agree or disagree with the authors that the problem of species extinction is serious? What pieces of evidence helped you draw your conclusion?
2. The authors use many facts, figures, and statistics to support their argument. But they do not, however, use any quotes. Which do you think would have been a more successful tool for supporting their argument—statistics or quotes? If your answer is statistics, explain which statistics you found most persuasive. If your answer is quotes, highlight places in the text where you think quotes would have bolstered the argument.

Species Extinction Is Not a Serious Problem

Bjørn Lomborg

In the following interview, Professor Bjørn Lomborg argues that species extinction is not a serious problem. Although he admits that some species extinction takes place because of human activity, he says the problem has been greatly exaggerated. Species are going extinct at a rate far less than commonly claimed, believes Lomborg. Furthermore, he argues, species extinction is a natural event that needs to be understood in the context of the evolution of the world. Lomborg concludes that sound environmental policies must be based on common sense rather than panic about species extinction.

Bjørn Lomborg is an associate professor of statistics at the University of Aarhus, Denmark.

Consider the Following Questions:

1. What is the extinction rate estimated by most experts for the next fifty years, as reported by Lomborg?
2. What is the "environmental litany," as explained by Lomborg?
3. Why does Lomborg believe that panic about the environment is dangerous?

Bjørn Lomborg, "Crisis Interviews Bjørn Lomborg," *Crisis Magazine*, April 1, 2004. Copyright © 2004 *Crisis Magazine*. All rights reserved. Reproduced by permission of www.crisismagazine.com.

Crisis: In your book, you mention what you refer to as the "environmental litany." What is this?

Bjørn Lomborg: It's the idea that everything is getting worse. That air pollution is getting worse, that there's not enough food, that we're despoiling the soil, that we're creating a world where things are going to hell and that—in the long term—we won't be able to sustain ourselves.

This is the common belief.

Definitely. And I document this with numerous quotes from a lot of different people. While this is how the issues are generally portrayed, it's wrong and it's not helping anyone understand them better. In reality, things are moving in the *right* direction. It's not getting worse and worse.

Letting Species Go

Extinction is a normal part of the natural evolutionary process. . . . Failure to recognize this phenomena will result in wasting expertise and money on recovery programs doomed to failure by this natural process while people lose their jobs and go hungry.

T. R. Mader, "Endangered Species Act:Flawed Law," Abundant Wildlife Society of North America, March 11, 2004. www.aws.vcn.com/flawed/htm.

"We Have Always Lost Species"

Give us a specific example of how your research contradicted one of the common environmental planks. Let's take biodiversity—the notion that species are becoming extinct left and right. Obviously, there are species that are disappearing, but is this the epidemic so often portrayed by activists?

We *are* causing some species extinction, simply because we have such a large presence in the world. So the discussion here is not whether or not it's happening—it is, and we need to face up to it. But we also need to get a sense of proportion in this. Where should we spend our limited resources? What kinds of priorities should we have?

But the common claim that we're going to lose anywhere from 25 to 50 percent of all species in our lifetimes is simply not true. It's not backed up by the data that we have. We've always lost species and we're losing more now than ever

The panda is an example of an endangered species that is slowly climbing in population, due to special care and breeding, that will one day be far from extinction.

before. But most experts estimate around 0.7 percent over the next 50 years.

We Must Not Give In to Panic

Look, if someone tells us we're going to lose 25 to 50 percent of our species in the next 50 years, then we'll go into a panic mode and will reach for any possible solution. After all, if that were true, it would be catastrophic.

A planet-changing phenomenon. . .

Right. And we'd need to go into an emergency mode. On the other hand, a loss of 0.7 percent is a problem—no question. But it's one problem among many problems. And there are

A sea turtle finds its way to the sea after being released from captivity.

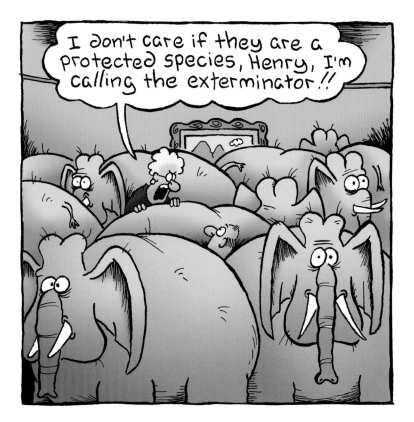

other problems that may be more pressing. This is where prioritization comes into play.

The analogy I use is this: Imagine someone puts a gun to your head and tells you to do something. If that happened, you'd do it quickly, without thinking. You act out of a panic. This is what we must not do, or we're going to make mistakes.

There's no environmental gun to our head?

Right.

Getting Our Environmental Problems Straight

As a statistician, you can look at the big picture—you can crunch the numbers. But the environmental scientists are experts in their fields. They can pick up nuances that may be missed in the big picture. How is your macro-view different from what they're seeing? Surely, they're not lying about what they're reporting.

No, of course not. But everyone thinks that his own interest is the most important thing. That's a very common thing. Before I started doing this, I was working on game theory and computer simulation. Possibly a couple hundred people in the world really cared about what that was. And yet, I thought that was one of the really important areas of study. It's natural.

And so biologists feel uncomfortable when someone comes along and says, "Sure, we're losing species and that's a problem. But how does that problem compare to some of the others we've got? How big a problem is this really?" This question is outside their scope of discussion, and I understand that. But in a political society, we need to have those kinds of discussions. Because we're prioritizing between a lot of different problems. We only have so many resources to address these issues.

Analyze the Essay:

1. In this essay, Bjørn Lomborg acknowledges that human activity is causing species extinction. Is this claim inconsistent with his overall argument? Why or why not?

2. Both Bjørn Lomborg and the authors of the previous viewpoint state that species extinction is a natural event that has always occurred. Based on what you know of this subject, at what point does species extinction begin to be an unnatural event? Explain your answer in full.

The Endangered Species Act Is Effective

Defenders of Wildlife

In the following viewpoint, the nature organization Defenders of Wildlife discusses positive effects the Endangered Species Act has had on endangered species. The authors detail seven endangered species that have been helped by the Act. Among other improvements, the Endangered Species Act has helped provide protection for animals' habitat; pressure industries to make their tools and equipment more animal-friendly; and reduce the use of harmful pesticides. Together these actions have protected endangered species and allowed them to bounce back from near extinction. For these reasons, they conclude, the Endangered Species Act should be regarded as an important tool for saving threatened wildlife.

Defenders of Wildlife is a non-profit organization dedicated to the protection of all native wild animals and plants in their natural habitats.

Consider the Following Questions:

1. According to the authors, how many of the 1800 species protected by the Endangered Species Act have succumbed to extinction?
2. How has the Endangered Species Act helped preserve sea turtles, as reported by Defenders of Wildlife?
3. How has the Aleutian Canada goose population changed from the mid-1970s, according to the authors?

Defenders of Wildlife, The Endangered Species Act, "Thirty Years of Success," 2004.
Copyright © 2006 Defenders of Wildlife. Reproduced by permission.

For more than 30 years, the Endangered Species Act has helped prevent the extinction of our nation's wildlife treasures. Because of the Act, beloved symbols of America such as the bald eagle, the Florida manatee and the California condor are all thriving.

Saving Species for Over 30 Years

Only nine of the 1,800 species currently protected by the Act have been declared extinct since the Act was signed into law in 1973, an astonishing success rate, making the Act a true symbol of our nation's successful commitment to protecting our natural heritage for future generations. It is also an example of the progress that can be made when communities work together to conserve their local wildlife and habitat.

Here are just a few examples of the creatures that have been saved by the Endangered Species Act and community efforts to implement it.

Bald Eagle Soaring

Today, the bald eagle once again soars through our nation's skies. But it wasn't always this way. Scientists estimate that more than 100,000 bald eagles once inhabited the United States, but only a few hundred nesting pairs could be found in the lower 48 states by the mid-1970s. Habitat destruction, trophy hunting and pesticide use had all taken their toll. America was slowly losing its national symbol.

The bald eagle was one of the first species listed under the Endangered Species Act, and in 1973 an aggressive recovery program was put in place. Universities, nonprofit organizations and federal agencies joined together to protect the eagle. Today there are more than 6,000 nesting pairs in the lower 48 states, making the bald eagle one of the Endangered Species Act's greatest success stories.

Improving Shrimp Nets to Save Turtles

All seven existing species of sea turtle face threats from the commercial fishing industry. Often they are caught up in tuna nets or other fishing gear, which can take a heavy toll on turtle populations. In the Gulf of Mexico and in the Atlantic, however, there has been success protecting these species, some of the oldest creatures on Earth.

Under the auspices of the Endangered Species Act, nongovernmental organizations have banded together to work with the shrimp industry and the National Marine Fisheries Service to develop turtle excluder devices (TEDs) for shrimp nets. These innovative devices help turtles find their way out of shrimp nets, allowing the shrimp industry to continue to prosper even as the turtle population begins to recover. TEDs have been very successful in reducing bycatch of smaller sea turtles like the Kemps Ridley turtle, with very little cost to shrimp vessels.

The Endangered Species Act has had positive effects on endangered species such as the sage grouse.

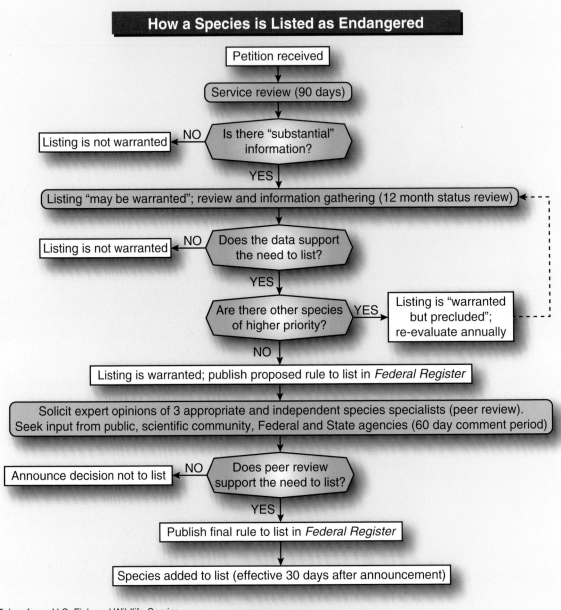

How a Species is Listed as Endangered

Petition received

Service review (90 days)

Is there "substantial" information? — NO → Listing is not warranted

YES

Listing "may be warranted"; review and information gathering (12 month status review)

Does the data support the need to list? — NO → Listing is not warranted

YES

Are there other species of higher priority? — YES → Listing is "warranted but precluded"; re-evaluate annually

NO

Listing is warranted; publish proposed rule to list in *Federal Register*

Solicit expert opinions of 3 appropriate and independent species specialists (peer review). Seek input from public, scientific community, Federal and State agencies (60 day comment period)

Does peer review support the need to list? — NO → Announce decision not to list

YES

Publish final rule to list in *Federal Register*

Species added to list (effective 30 days after announcement)

Taken from: U.S. Fish and Wildlife Service

As a result of these successes, efforts are now under-way to increase the size of TED openings to accommodate endangered leatherbacks and other large turtles, and to encourage the adoption of TED technology throughout their habitat.

Marching Back from the Brink

Before 1940, there were an estimated 3,875 pairs of breeding peregrine falcons in North America. In the 1940s, however, this magnificent raptor started suffering significant declines due to indiscriminate use of the pesticide DDT. By 1970, only 10 to 20 percent of the historic falcon population remained and the falcon was listed as an endangered species.

Fortunately, the pesticide DDT was banned in 1972, and by 1997, there were more than 1,400 pairs of peregrines in North America, more than double the original recovery goal of 631 pairs. These recovery efforts were deemed so success-ful that the U.S. Fish and Wildlife Service removed the peregrine falcon from the list of endangered species in August 1999.

The gray wolf once occupied most of the lower 48 states, from the Northeast to the Pacific Coast. But by the early 1900s habitat loss, hunting and human persecution had decimated the wolf's numbers. By the mid-1900s, gray wolves in the lower 48 could only be found in the Great Lakes region, where just a few hundred of these animals lived.

In 1974, gray wolves were given protection under the Endangered Species Act and their populations slowly began to climb. In 1995, wolves were reintroduced into the

Saving Species for More Than Thirty Years

There can be no denying that, with the Endangered Species Act's help, hundreds of species have been rescued from the catastrophic permanence of extinction.

Jamie Rappaport Clark, testimony before the U.S. Senate Subcommittee on Fisheries, Wildlife, and Water, Committee on the Environment and Public Works, Washington DC, May 19, 2005.

Yellowstone ecosystem, where they have thrived and provided numerous ecological and economic benefits to the region. Today, the gray wolf, one of the most recognizable symbols of the American wilderness, continues its march back from the brink of extinction as scientists, tourists and communities across the country continue to marvel at the resilience of this magnificent creature.

The Needs of Animals and Humans

The Aleutian Canada goose population had dwindled to just a few hundred in the mid-1970s, but current population estimates run as high as 100,000 birds. This improvement was due to an innovative effort that spanned from the Aleutian Islands in Alaska, where the birds breed, along the Oregon coast, a staging area for spring migration, and into California's San Joaquin and Sacramento valleys, where they spend the winter.

Through partnerships with landowners, conservation organizations and federal and state government agencies, biologists were able to protect geese through predator control in breeding grounds and through partnerships with local landowners to protect and manage land needed for winter habitat.

Now, the Aleutian Canada goose has been declared fully recovered and state officials continue to work with local landowners to balance the needs of farmers and the birds.

The Florida manatee is one of the most endangered marine mammals in the coastal waters of the United States today. It is a gentle sea cow that is often mortally wounded by high-speed recreational boats and threatened by the loss of bottom grasses, its preferred food.

In 1979, the U.S. Fish and Wildlife Service identified special refuges and established a program to allow human use of those areas while encouraging the recovery of the threatened manatee. Today, boaters know to be on the lookout

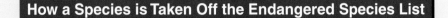

How a Species is Taken Off the Endangered Species List

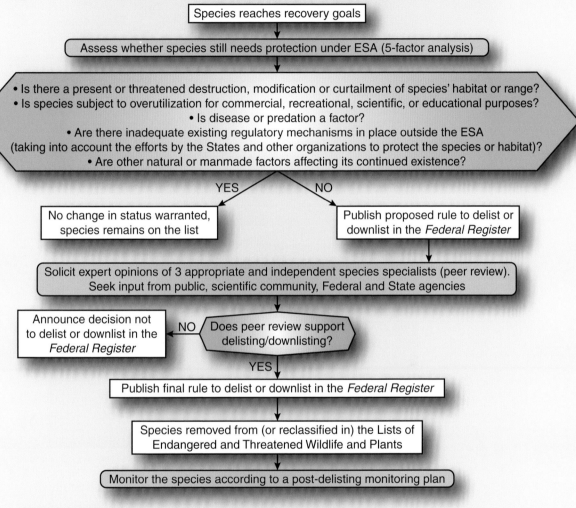

Species reaches recovery goals

Assess whether species still needs protection under ESA (5-factor analysis)

- Is there a present or threatened destruction, modification or curtailment of species' habitat or range?
- Is species subject to overutilization for commercial, recreational, scientific, or educational purposes?
- Is disease or predation a factor?
- Are there inadequate existing regulatory mechanisms in place outside the ESA (taking into account the efforts by the States and other organizations to protect the species or habitat)?
- Are other natural or manmade factors affecting its continued existence?

YES — No change in status warranted, species remains on the list

NO — Publish proposed rule to delist or downlist in the *Federal Register*

Solicit expert opinions of 3 appropriate and independent species specialists (peer review). Seek input from public, scientific community, Federal and State agencies

Does peer review support delisting/downlisting?

NO — Announce decision not to delist or downlist in the *Federal Register*

YES

Publish final rule to delist or downlist in the *Federal Register*

Species removed from (or reclassified in) the Lists of Endangered and Threatened Wildlife and Plants

Monitor the species according to a post-delisting monitoring plan

Source: U.S. Fish and Wildlife Service

The yellow-billed loon is an example of an endangered species bouncing back from extinction.

for manatees and abide by "slow" zones to avoid critically injuring these gentle giants. Though still at-risk, the manatee is around today largely due to the Endangered Species Act.

Keep the ESA Strong

The southern sea otter was listed as threatened under the Endangered Species Act in 1977. Under the Act's Section 7 consultation process, the Minerals Management Service and the U.S. Coast Guard worked with the U.S. Fish and

Wildlife Service to recover the southern sea otter. This process provided valuable guidance on avoiding otter deaths due to offshore oil development and oil tanker traffic, while still allowing those activities to continue. As a result of recovery planning, the sea otter population is increasing. Various marine mammals and sea birds have also been conserved by protecting the sea otter, one of nature's keystone species. The animal remains a major tourist attraction in California's waters, providing economic benefits to local communities.

These are just a few of the species that are around today because of the Endangered Species Act and people like you who get involved to help ensure the Act stays strong.

Analyze the Essay:

1. In this viewpoint, the authors use specific language to make their points. For example, they refer to manatees as "gentle giants" and describe how thanks to the ESA, Americans "continue to marvel at the resilience of this magnificent creature [the gray wolf]." What tone does using such language give the essay? What emotions does it evoke in you? Do you find these types of descriptions moving or off-putting? Explain your answer in detail.

2. The authors of this viewpoint argue that the Endangered Species Act has an "astonishing success rate." How do you think the author of the following viewpoint, T. R. Mader of the Abundant Wildlife Society of North America, would respond to such a claim?

The Endangered Species Act Is Not Effective

Abundant Wildlife Society of North America

In the following viewpoint, author T. R. Mader argues the Endangered Species Act requires Americans to spend too much money saving animals at the expense of human rights. Saving some endangered species costs millions of dollars which, in Mader's opinion, is not worth the saving of an animal. Mader also takes issue with the fact that building development projects have been halted or abandoned because of harm that could have been done to an endangered species. He argues that people have the right to build on or sell their land, and the Endangered Species Act should not interfere with that right. Species extinction is a natural part of life, argues Mader. He therefore concludes the Endangered Species Act interferes with natural evolutionary processes and unfairly trumps the rights of humans.

T. R. Mader is the research director of the Abundant Wildlife Society of North America, from which this viewpoint was taken.

Consider the Following Questions:

1. Why does the author believe the desert tortoise should not receive protection under the Endangered Species Act?
2. What punishment did a Texas man receive for killing an endangered whooping crane, as reported by Mader?
3. What constitutional rights does the Endangered Species Act deprive people of, in Mader's view?

T. R. Mader, "Endangered Species Act: Flawed Law," Abundant Wildlife Society of North America, March 11, 2004. Reproduced by permission.

We believe care and concern for the environment and our wildlife is important. Due to that importance, the Endangered Species Act (ESA) was passed into law with the best of intentions—to save endangered species of animals and plants from extinction.

Unfortunately, it's had little success. However, the ESA has become a most effective tool in the hands of the preservationist and those intent on destroying the livelihoods of millions of Americans.

Choosing Animals Over People
DID YOU KNOW:

- the desert tortoise is listed on the (ESA) when there are an estimated 3 million tortoises in the desert and another 100,000 in captivity?. . .
- a pond weed, which was found on private land in Texas, was petitioned for listing on the ESA without the knowledge of the land owner. U.S. Fish and Wildlife Service (FWS) workers simply trespassed to conduct their research studies.
- a snail prevented a retired veteran in Kanab, Utah from building a recreational vehicle park and tourist site on his own property? The FWS alleged an endangered snail (kanab amber snail) was found on his property. An "emergency" listing of the snail was obtained. The veteran was told he could not use his property and has no option but to sell it to the government.
- shrimpers in the gulf coast states of Texas and Louisiana are being harassed by the National Marine Fisheries Service (NMFS) over a non-native sea turtle? Yes, that's right, the Kemp's Ridley sea turtle does not nest in the United States, but in Mexico. Government biologists bring the eggs to the U.S., hatch them in Texas and release them in the Gulf of Mexico. The NMFS has conducted over 1,100 indiscriminate searches of shrimper's boats under the guise of turtle protection. Not one turtle

U.S. Representative Dennis Cardoza (front) answers a question about revising the Endangered Species Act during a conference.

has been found on these boats. Fines for not having a Turtle Excluding Device (TED) range from $8000 to $25,000. . . .

Spending Millions . . . For What?

- The sockeye salmon is listed as endangered on the Colombia, Snake and Salmon Rivers? This ESA listing affects 900 miles of rivers systems. This recovery program will cost between $200 million and $1 billion dollars in the next five years—a price to be paid by electricity ratepayers, farmers, river operators and commercial fishermen.
- The Clarkea Australia, a small one to two inch high plant, has shut down logging in parts of California? It's not because the plant is in the logging areas per se, but because the jobs were located in areas where the Forest Service said there "might" be Clarkea Australia.

Mind you, this tenacious little plant will grow in skidder tracks, but that doesn't matter.

- The USFWS spent over $102 million in fiscal year 1990 on threatened and endangered species? The 10 species with the highest reported expenditures were: northern spotted owl ($9.7 million); least bell's vireo [small, green bird similar to the warbler] ($9.2 million); grizzly bear ($5.9 million); red cockaded woodpecker ($5.2 million); Florida panther ($4.1 million); Mojave desert tortoise ($4.1 million); bald eagle ($3.5 million); ocelot ($3 million); jaguarundi [slender, short-legged wildcat] ($2.9 million); American Peregrine falcon (2.9 million). The highest costing bug was the valley elderberry longhorn beetle ($952,000) and the highest plant was the northern wild monkshood ($226,000). Note: These figures are not the total cost, only what can be itemized by species.

- the snail darter, which was used to hold up construction of Tennessee Valley Authority's (TVA) Tellico Dam, was known to exist in other areas and yet the FWS listed it on the ESA, claiming it was nearly extinct? . . .
- two California condors were released in January 1992? What did recovery cost? Nearly 30 years preparation and $25 million dollars!

Taking Private Property

- a Texas man killed an endangered whooping crane and was imprisoned for six months and fined over $200,000?
- a Maryland couple could not prevent erosion to their home, which was built on a 60 foot cliff overlooking Chesapeake Bay, because it might harm a bug? That's right—the Puritan Tiger Beetle to be exact. An official from the Maryland Natural Heritage Program stated that protecting bug habitat was more important than protecting the couple's home. A letter to the governor changed nothing, the beetle's rights came first! . . .
- government officials designated 6.9 million acres of forest in the Pacific Northwest to be set aside for the spotted owl? (6.9 million acres is larger than the states of Massachusetts and Rhode Island combined.) The government's estimate of job loss is 33,000 jobs. Private sources say 60,000 jobs is more accurate. Additionally, landowners of some three million acres in the Pacific Northwest were told they could not harvest timber on their own land due to the presence of the northern spotted owl, even though seven million acres of wilderness already exists for the owl. . . .
- the Colombia white-tailed deer has been listed as endangered for years and millions have been spent on its recovery? Studies reveal that the deer is "genetically a plain jane whitetail deer." . . .

- in spite of the best intentions and million upon millions of dollars spent, the Endangered Species Act (ESA) is a dismal failure, in terms of species recovery? . . .

Trampling Peoples' Rights for the Sake of Animals

The Endangered Species Act (ESA) has been used to:

1. Lock up vast areas of land from commodity use, i.e. the northern spotted owl used to shut down timber harvest in the Pacific Northwest.

2. Deprive an individual of their constitutional right of protection of private property, i.e. threat of $100,000 fine and mandatory prison sentence for killing an endangered wolf killing ones' livestock.

3. Deprive one of their property without just compensation, i.e. restriction on use and/ or acquisition of land as critical habitat for endangered species.

An Abused Law

Success stories in species recovery due to the Endangered Species Act are few and far between. The law has fallen victim to unintended consequences, partisan politics, and counter-productive lawsuits filed by environmental organizations.

Richard W. Pombo, "The ESA at 30: Time for Congress to Update and Strengthen the Law," www.cdfe.org, 2005.

The Endangered Species Act Is Broken

The following changes, in order to bring balance and to put the human factor back into the ESA, are necessary: . . .

The socio-economic impacts of a listing must be considered. The current law makes no such consideration.

Problem Example: Land values in an area of Texas fell an estimated $300 million dollars due to an ESA listing of a songbird—the golden-cheeked warbler.

Also, the impacts of spotted owl listing on the timber industry in the Pacific Northwest. *The Wall Street Journal* reported a 25% cost increase in wood products which was

A protestor rallies against the Endangered Species Act at a high school in New Mexico near the Rio Grande.

directly related to the listing of the spotted owl. Thus, the nation, not just loggers, are impacted by the ESA listing of the spotted owl.

There must be just compensation on any taking of private property. The constitutional rights of citizens must be protected.

Individuals must have the right to protect their livelihoods and control endangered species threatening their livelihoods.

Problem Example: Endangered wolves, grizzly bears or eagles killing livestock cannot be killed by the owner of the livestock. A federal judge has ruled that a person does not have the constitutional right to protect their property from an endangered species. In 1990, over 7,500 sheep and lambs were killed by eagles in the states of Wyoming, Montana and Colorado alone.

Extinction Is a Normal Part of Life

The ESA must recognize that extinction is a normal part of the natural evolutionary process. The fossil record makes this abundantly clear. Failure to recognize this phenomena will result in wasting expertise and money on recovery programs doomed to failure by this natural process while people lose their jobs and go hungry.

Time and expenditure limits must be placed on studies and recovery plans. The American taxpayer is entitled to fiscal responsibility of government agencies directed to saving endangered species.

Analyze the Essay:

1. In this viewpoint, T. R. Mader brings up the example of the Colombia white-tailed deer, arguing it is not worth being protected because it is "genetically plain." What is your opinion of this idea? Are only exotic species worthy of being protected, or should all endangered animals be protected, even if there is nothing genetically special or unique about them? Explain your answer.

2. Defenders of Wildlife, the authors of the previous viewpoint, discusses how the Endangered Species Act helped the shrimp industry reform its nets so endangered sea turtles would not get caught in them. In this viewpoint, T. R. Mader argues that shrimpers have been "harassed" and have had to pay large fines for not having the turtle-excluding nets. Note how each author describes the situation. What are the differences in each description? With which author do you agree on this particular issue? Should shrimp boats be encouraged to reduce the harm done to sea turtles, or does such an action constitute harassment and cost too much money? Support your answer using evidence from the text.

Cloning Can Save Endangered Species

Audubon Nature Institute

Cloning can help save endangered species by artificially adding more numbers to a species' population, argue the authors of the following viewpoint. It can also help enlarge the genetic diversity of small animal populations, which can prevent a dwindling population from inbreeding and suffering from birth defects and other species-threatening health problems. Furthermore, the authors claim that cloning can help eliminate disease in an endangered species by cloning only the healthy and strongest animals. For these reasons the authors conclude that cloning, along with habitat restoration and other efforts, can help prevent species extinction.

This viewpoint was published by the Audubon Center for Research of Endangered Species, a wing of the Audubon Nature Institute, a conservation organization based in Louisiana.

Consider the Following Questions:

1. Describe how the cat Ditteaux was created.
2. In what way can cloning be like a "booster shot" to a species, according to the authors?
3. What does the word "multi-faceted" mean in the context of the viewpoint?

Audubon Nature Institute, "Nuclear Transfer (Cloning)," Audubon Center for Research for Endangered Species, 2006. Copyright © 2006 Audubon Nature Institute. Reproduced by permission.

The world's first cloned endangered African wildcat was born in New Orleans, Louisiana. The cat was born as a result of groundbreaking research conducted at Audubon Nature Institute's Research Center by scientists from Audubon Center for Research of Endangered Species and Louisiana State University.

The kitten is the first cloned wild carnivore. Born to a common domestic housecat on August 6, 2003, the kitten was created using frozen/thawed genetic material from the African wildcat Jazz, who was also born to a domestic cat, but as a result of a different kind of procedure, the first successful in vitro fertilized frozen/thawed embryo transfer.

The birth of Jazz in November, 1999, at Audubon Center for Research of Endangered Species made headlines around the world.

Cloning Can Save Endangered Species

Cloning and other assisted reproduction technologies can benefit endangered species by increasing the potential of boosting their numbers, preserving and propagating species that reproduce poorly in zoos. This will help to maintain genetic diversity of endangered species. Cloning can introduce new genes back into the gene pool of species that have few remaining animals. In addition, freezing this genetic material in the Frozen Zoo can keep the cells viable for an indefinite period of time.

"Here in Louisiana, scientists are growing ever closer to unlocking the secrets that could make extinction extinct," said Ron Forman, President and CEO of Audubon Nature Institute of New Orleans. "These are significant births representing important steps in our understanding of how technology can be engaged to help save endangered

---

Preserving Species for Tomorrow's World

What if 100 years from now people finally figure out how to save the habitats, but there are no animals? [Cloning] is part of the answer.

Audubon Nature Institute's Center for Research of Endangered Species spokeswoman Sarah Burnette quoted in Amy Hembree. "Cloning Is No Extinction Panacea," *Wired*, February 13, 2001, p. 2.

species. Audubon Nature Institute is proud to be a pioneer in this area, and proud of our partnerships, like that with Louisiana State University, which enable us to continue this innovative work.". . .

Though a controversial method, cloning could be the answer to saving endangered species.

Winning the Battle Against Extinction

To create the cloned embryo, scientists took tissue samples from the male African wildcat, Jazz. These cells were grown in tissue culture to provide a supply of thousands of cells, each with the wildcat's DNA. The cells were frozen in the Frozen Zoo. Then, DNA was removed from an egg of a domestic cat. Frozen-thawed cells from Jazz were inserted into the domestic cat egg cells. The egg was exposed to an electric current, causing the new DNA to fuse with the egg, which divided to become an embryo. The embryo was then implanted into the uterus of a domestic cat surrogate, who

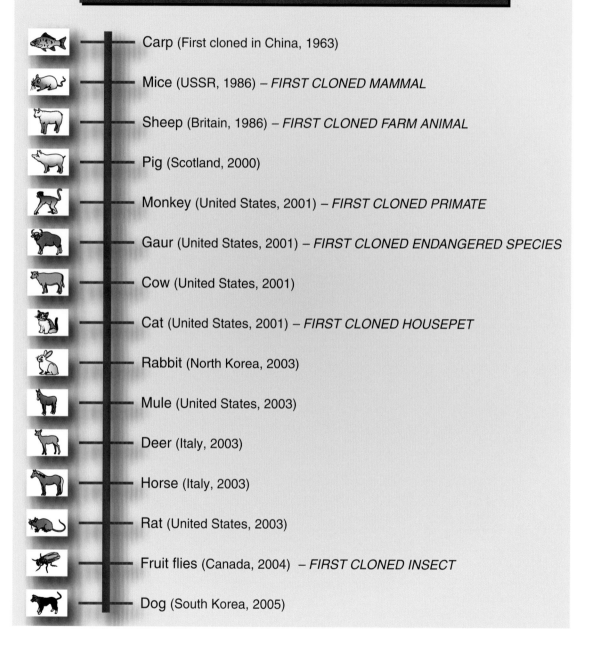

Successfully Cloned Animals

Carp (First cloned in China, 1963)

Mice (USSR, 1986) – *FIRST CLONED MAMMAL*

Sheep (Britain, 1986) – *FIRST CLONED FARM ANIMAL*

Pig (Scotland, 2000)

Monkey (United States, 2001) – *FIRST CLONED PRIMATE*

Gaur (United States, 2001) – *FIRST CLONED ENDANGERED SPECIES*

Cow (United States, 2001)

Cat (United States, 2001) – *FIRST CLONED HOUSEPET*

Rabbit (North Korea, 2003)

Mule (United States, 2003)

Deer (Italy, 2003)

Horse (Italy, 2003)

Rat (United States, 2003)

Fruit flies (Canada, 2004) – *FIRST CLONED INSECT*

Dog (South Korea, 2005)

went on to have a normal pregnancy before giving birth to the cloned kitten.

"Drs. [Earle] Pope and [Martha C.] Gomez achieved this milestone through persistence and teamwork," said Dr. Dresser. "Technology alone will not be enough to save endangered species, but it's impossible to win the battle against extinction without it. Now we have new tools we can use to keep hope alive for species facing dramatically dwindling numbers. Working with all the resources we have at our disposal, we have a chance to rescue animals from the brink of extinction."

The kitten, named Ditteaux, was born to domestic cat Brooke. The kitten is being cared for and nursed by the surrogate mother. Jazz, the headline-grabbing African wildcat, continues to live at Audubon Center for Research of Endangered Species in New Orleans. His surrogate mother, domestic cat Cayenne, was adopted by Dr. Pope. The two wildcats who donated the sperm and egg to create Jazz are living at the research center as well. . . .

To Preserve and Propagate

Genetic diversity of small animal populations can be increased [with cloning]. As the population of an endangered species decreases, its bloodlines become more inbred, rendering the animals more vulnerable to birth defects and other health problems. Clones of healthy animals can be introduced into wild populations and give a "booster shot" of fresh genetic material to a species undergoing a lost genetic diversity.

Clones of endangered species can help to preserve and propagate species that reproduce poorly in captivity.

Researchers studying the evolution of a species will have access to a larger population sample without having to go into the field to collect samples from many species.

Two female cloned wolves show the possibilities that cloning has to offer those species facing extinction.

The Role of Biotechnologies

Cloning, artificial insemination, transgenic science and in vitro fertilization are all new biotechnologies which have appeared relatively recently in the field of assisted reproduction. All are being developed for use with domestic animals such as cattle, as well as for use with endangered species. While these technologies seemed far-fetched and generated much public discussion when first introduced, they are routine today and are viewed as part of the reproductive "toolkit." When applied in conjunction with traditional conservation tools such as preservation of habitat and animal population management in captivity and in the wild, these new biotechnologies can play a pivotal role in the battle against extinction.

Scientists at Audubon Center for Research of Endangered Species, the research component of Audubon Nature Institute of New Orleans, Louisiana, are working with these technologies to help endangered species. In doing so, Audubon Nature Institute scientists and staff are bound to observe the most humane standards when working with the animals in their care. . . .

These technologies can benefit endangered species by increasing the potential for boosting their numbers, preserving and propagating species, helping to maintain genetic diversity. Cloning can introduce new genes back into the pool of species that have few remaining animals. Also, cloning can help to eliminate disease in a population by cloning only the disease-free animals. . . .

Cloning Is One Part of the Solution

[Some might say,] *Wouldn't it be better to be saving habitat?* Extinction is a multi-faceted problem that requires a coordinated, strategic response. Preserving habitat is an extremely important tool in this battle, but it is not the only tool and saving habitat alone will not solve the problem. At Audubon Center for Research of Endangered Species, we focus on the science of reproduction, developing a safety net outside of the unstable political arena in many developing countries to help save endangered species. The money used to support the reproduction research to provide this safety net are not available for saving habitat, even in the U.S., so we are not put into the position of having to make the choice. With the funding that is available to us, we must focus our research on the laboratory science.

[Some might say,] *Isn't this a lot like playing God?* Humans have already disturbed the natural order more than any other species in the history of the world. We should utilize whatever methods we have to reverse some of the damage we have already done and give the people of the future options for working with wildlife. Man plays God all of the time when he chooses to destroy the planet to make more room for our species!

Cloning to Save Endangered Species Appeals to More Americans

A series of polls revealed that Americans favored cloning animals if it helped save endangered species.

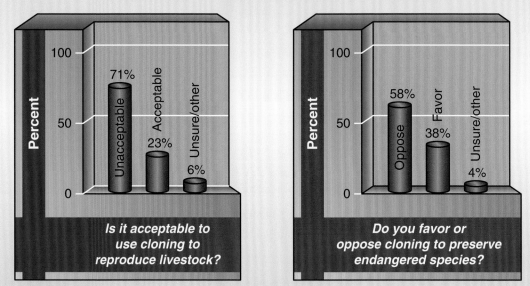

Taken from: Carol Tucker Foreman, Consumer Federation of America

Analyze the Essay:

1. How do the authors answer criticisms that cloning animals is akin to playing God? Do you agree with their position? Why or why not?
2. Examine the quotations included in this essay. Who was quoted? What qualifications do they have? Are they authorities in their field? Where were the quotes positioned in the piece? How did they enliven the essay?

Improved Pharmaceuticals Can Save Endangered Species

J.D. Smith

In many cultures, endangered species such as bears, bats, or rhinoceroses are hunted and eaten because people believe they have medicinal properties. Some people believe, for example, that eating the Philippine fruit bat will improve a man's sexual performance. In the following viewpoint, J.D. Smith suggests that pharmaceuticals, such as the erectile dysfunction drug Viagra, could be distributed around the world to replace the need to hunt endangered species for this purpose. If people had a pill to take for such needs, they wouldn't need to turn to poachers, who in turn wouldn't need to hunt endangered species to sell. Smith concludes that a worldwide pharmaceutical distribution program could become one of the most successful conservation efforts ever undertaken.

J. D. Smith is a writer, editor, and poet in Washington, D.C. He has published two books of poems, including *Settling for Beauty*.

Consider the Following Questions:

1. What are three creatures the author says are hunted for their aphrodisiacal properties?
2. According to the author, what are two tragedies that result from using animal-based remedies?
3. Who is Alan "Ace" Greenberg and what program did he spearhead, as reported by the author?

J. D. Smith, "An Immodest Proposal," *Grist Magazine*, March 22, 2005. Copyright © 2005 *Grist Magazine, Inc.* All rights reserved. Reproduced by permission.

Quick: what do sea turtles, black bears, and Philippine fruit bats have in common?

At first glance, not much. They don't look alike, and they have very different ranges and habitats. In fact, one would be hard-pressed even to find them on any of the same guest lists.

But these creatures share one very important trait. Along with seahorses, rhinoceroses, and macaques, they are all hunted, sold, and consumed for use in potions and dishes with alleged "aphrodisiacal properties." For men. And I think we know what that means.

Endangered Species Are Killed for Medicinal Properties

In a more perfect world, we men might be willing to age gracefully and hang up—well, whatever it is we hang up, say, spurs—and retire from certain pleasures of the flesh. When that happens, though, men will be too distracted to care. We'll be busy watching pigs fly.

Until that day arrives, there will be a market for products that enhance "male performance" (presumably not in rugby). In Asia and Central America, among other places, this means resorting to traditional, animal-based remedies. Two tragedies can result. The first is personal: they may not work. The second is even, ahem, greater: threatened species are being hunted to extinction, with untold consequences for ecosystems and economies.

As experts in international development know, however, this is generally not a matter of good guys and bad guys, black hats and white. Poachers, often poor and uneducated, are simply trying to make a living

Substituting Modern Medicine for Endangered Species

Bats are being killed for another purpose . . . for their flesh as food, medicine and aphrodisiac potions. The Chinese believe that bat meat can cure asthma, kidney ailments and treat general malaise. (One can at least understand the killing of bats or other animals for food in times of famine but it is very hard to condone the eating of bat meat for aphrodisiac purposes or to treat ailments that appear to have their root causes in our modern day diets and lifestyle.)"

Lim Gaik Kee, "No Bats, No Durians," *Nature Watch*, Vol. 6 No. 2 Apr–Jun 98.

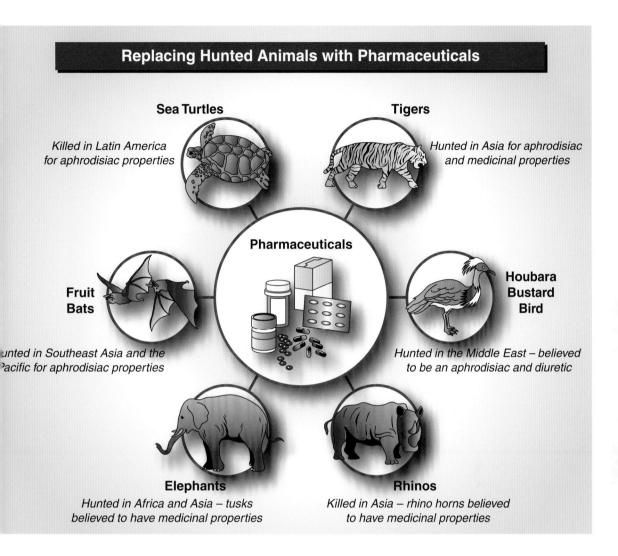

Replacing Hunted Animals with Pharmaceuticals

Sea Turtles
Killed in Latin America for aphrodisiac properties

Tigers
Hunted in Asia for aphrodisiac and medicinal properties

Pharmaceuticals

Fruit Bats
...unted in Southeast Asia and the Pacific for aphrodisiac properties

Houbara Bustard Bird
Hunted in the Middle East – believed to be an aphrodisiac and diuretic

Elephants
Hunted in Africa and Asia – tusks believed to have medicinal properties

Rhinos
Killed in Asia – rhino horns believed to have medicinal properties

by meeting a demand. If the market for their contraband product dries up, or if alternative livelihoods are available, they might well find other work.

Pharmaceuticals Can Replace Natural Medicines

Of course, this is easier said than done. Behavior and culture take time to change, and there is no silver bullet. There is, however, a little blue pill.

Many animals, such as the black bear, are hunted for pharmaceutical uses, which can lead to extinction.

Yupper. That one. Sildenafil citrate, though no one calls it that. It is currently sold by Pfizer (in which I have no stock) under the name of Viagra, but even after the patent expires the name seems likely to remain in the language, like Kleenex or Xerox, as the term for a whole product category and not just one brand.

Of course, there are now other products for the treatment of erectile dysfunction, which goes by the friendly acronym ED. (This sounds like someone you might play poker with once a week.) Treatments for our pal ED now include Bayer and GlaxoSmithKline's Levitra (vardenafil hydrochloride), a brand name derived from the Latin root of the verb "to raise," and ICOS and Eli Lilly's Cialis (tadalafil), which sounds like an MTV VJ from the late 1980s. More brands are forthcoming and, as with Viagra, after the patent period expires, the eventual generic market for these drugs is expected to be sizeable.

Distribute Pharmaceuticals to Those Who Would Hunt

The implication is clear. If we want to save black bears and rhinos, we have to get these drugs into the hands of the people who would otherwise be paying for those animals' parts or doing the hunting for themselves.

Many can pay, and for them—and our endangered animal friends—liberalized trade and e-commerce have their advantages.

But those who can't pay shouldn't be left out. Responsibly packaged along with condoms, to prevent unwanted pregnancies and the spread of disease, a little pharmaceutical lift might brighten an aid recipient's day a wee bit more than the typical relief package of rice, beans, and cooking oil. Scented candles, of course, could be optional.

Due to the development of pharmaceuticals, endangered species such as the Indian rhinoceroses, hunted for its aphrodisiacal properties, might be saved from extinction.

A Revolutionary Conservation Effort

Believe it or not, there's a precedent for this. In 1998, Bear Stearns chair Alan "Ace" Greenberg (bless him) donated $1 million to New York's Hospital for Special Surgery to provide Viagra to men who otherwise couldn't afford it, when that was the only game in town. Whatever else the recipients of his largesse might be doing, they don't have to scour the alleys and backrooms of Manhattan in an attempt to score black-bear gall bladder, macaque meat, or powdered seahorse. Other potential donors (we're looking at you, Bill & Melinda Gates Foundation) could do the same for the developing world.

Of course, no proposal is perfect. Pharmaceutical manufacturing creates pollution in the form of smokestack emissions and runoff. And pharmaceutical use produces externalities: fluoxetine hydrochloride, the active ingredient in Prozac, has been detected in (probably cheerful) fish in urban waterways. While the effects of ED medications on aquatic life have not been studied extensively, one might have reason to believe that in some places the fish will really be jumpin'. The situation will need to be watched, though not too closely—that would be kind of creepy.

The private sector, governments, and NGOs all have roles to play in what could be one of the most important conservation initiatives of our time. Countless biotic and human communities could benefit.

And the old methods wouldn't be missed. As far as I can tell, no one is eating Philippine fruit bat for the taste.

Analyze the Essay:

1. In this essay, author J. D. Smith peppers his writing with playful phrases such as "We'll be busy watching pigs fly," "that would be kind of creepy," and "Yupper." How does this type of language affect the way you read his essay? Do you find it engaging or interesting? Or do you find it distracting and inappropriate? Explain your answer.

2. Smith mentions that even though it could help save endangered species, widespread distribution of Viagra could also have some damaging affects on the environment. What are these damaging effects? Do you think these environmental costs are worth saving endangered species? Why or why not?

Section Two: Model Essays and Writing Exercises

The Five-Paragraph Essay

An *essay* is a short piece of writing that discusses or analyzes one topic. The five-paragraph essay is a form commonly used in school assignments and tests. Every five-paragraph essay begins with an *introduction,* ends with a *conclusion,* and features three *supporting paragraphs* in the middle.

The Thesis Statement. The introduction includes the essay's thesis statement. The thesis statement presents the argument or point the author is trying to make about the topic. The essays in this book all have different thesis statements because they are making different arguments about endangered species.

The thesis statement should clearly tell the reader what the essay will be about. A focused thesis statement helps determine what will be in the essay; the subsequent paragraphs are spent developing and supporting its argument.

The Introduction. In addition to presenting the thesis statement, a well-written introductory paragraph captures the attention of the reader and explains why the topic being explored is important. It may provide the reader with background information on the subject matter or feature an anecdote that illustrates a point relevant to the topic. It could also present startling information that clarifies the point of the essay or put forth a contradictory position that the essay will refute. Further techniques for writing an introduction are found later in this section.

The Supporting Paragraphs. The introduction is then followed by three (or more) supporting paragraphs. These are the main body of the essay. Each paragraph presents and develops a *subtopic* that supports the essay's thesis statement. Each subtopic is then supported with its own facts, details, and examples. The writer can use various kinds of supporting material and details to back up the topic of each supporting paragraph. These may include statistics, quotations from people with special knowledge or expertise, historic facts, and anecdotes. A rule of writing is that specific and concrete examples are more convincing than vague, general, or unsupported assertions.

The Conclusion. The *conclusion* is the paragraph that closes the essay. Its function is to summarize or reiterate the main idea of the essay. It may recall an idea from the introduction or briefly examine the larger implications of the thesis. Because the conclusion is also the last chance a writer has to make an impression on the reader, it is important that it not simply repeat what has been presented elsewhere in the essay but close it in a clear, final, and memorable way.

Although the order of the essay's component paragraphs is important, they do not have to be written in the order presented here. Some writers like to decide on a thesis and write the introduction paragraph first. Other writers like to focus first on the body of the essay, and write the introduction and conclusion later.

Pitfalls to Avoid

When writing essays about controversial issues such as endangered species, it is important to remember that disputes over the material are common precisely because there are many different perspectives. Remember to state your arguments in careful and measured terms. Evaluate your topic fairly—avoid overstating negative qualities of one perspective or understating positive qualities of another. Use examples, facts, and details to support any assertions you make.

The Compare-and-Contrast Essay

The last section of this book provided you with samples of previously published writing on endangered species. All are persuasive, or opinion, essays that make certain arguments about various topics relating to endangered species. Most of them also compare and contrast different facts and figures to make their arguments. This section will focus on writing your own compare-and-contrast essay.

In terms of presenting information and making an argument, the compare-and-contrast method can be a very effective way to organize an essay. At the heart of the compare-and-contrast essay is the act of evaluating two or more issues, things, or ideas next to each other. Such side-by-side glances can often reveal aspects of one subject that might have gone unnoticed had it been evaluated by itself.

Ways to Structure Compare-and-Contrast Essays

There are two basic ways to structure your compare and contrast essay. You can either evaluate your subjects point by point, analyzing them together throughout the essay. Alternatively, you can evaluate your subjects separately, reserving the first half of the essay for one subject and the second half of the essay for the other. Sometimes you may find it is effective to mix these two approaches, but in general the form you choose will determine the overall structure, pacing, and flow of the essay.

Sometimes the compare-and-contrast essay can focus on either the similarities or the differences between your subjects. A comparison essay usually explores the similarities between two subjects, while a contrast essay focuses on their differences. You can compare your subjects solely in order to present their commonality, or you can contrast your subjects only in order to expose their fundamental differences. Of course, you can also compare and contrast in the same essay. This approach is useful when your subjects are not entirely similar or different, which is often the case. This method can be effective when attempting to define, analyze, or arrive at a more in-depth understanding of your subjects.

Compare-and-contrast essays can also have one of two purposes. They can be used to conduct objective, unbiased discussions of two or more subjects, or they can be useful for making persuasive arguments in which you attempt to convince the reader of something. The effect can be achieved by evaluating two subjects' advantages and disadvantages, or showing in what ways one is superior to another. Then you would advocate a course of action or express a preference for one over the other.

Tips to Remember

Regardless of what style of compare-and-contrast essay you choose, there are certain features common to all of them. For example, all compare-and-contrast essays focus on at least two subjects. Furthermore, all compare-and-contrast essays feature certain transitional words that signal a similarity or difference is being pointed out.

When writing compare-and-contrast essays it is important to choose two subjects that are comparable or contrastable. For example, you could write a simple compare-and-contrast essay that focuses on the similarities and differences of oranges and apples, or t-shirts and sweaters. You would not, however, want to set out to compare oranges and tables or t-shirts and rice. The subjects you choose to compare or contrast must be linked in a basic way so that they warrant an examination. In terms of endangered species, it makes sense to compare and contrast different methods of preserving endangered species. It would not, however, make sense to compare the efficacy of preserving habitat to the life cycle of animals that live on the land because they are inherently different subjects.

In the following section you will read some model essays on endangered species that use compare-and-contrast arguments. You will also complete exercises that will help you write your own.

Words and Phrases Common in Compare-and-Contrast Essays

additionally
also; too
alternatively
as well as
conversely
equally
from this perspective
furthermore
however
in comparison
in contrast
in the same way
likewise
moreover
on the contrary
on the other hand
similarly
then again

What Makes a Species Endangered?

Editor's Notes A compare-and-contrast essay can be written in several different ways. One way is to describe thing or argument A, describe thing or argument B, and then compare them. Another way is to analyze two subjects' similarities or differences. The following five-paragraph essay does just that: it analyzes the differences between healthy and endangered species. The essay is structured as a five-paragraph essay in which each paragraph contributes a supporting piece of evidence to develop the argument.

The notes in the margin point out key features of the essay, and will help you understand how the essay is organized. Also note that all sources are cited using Modern Language Association (MLA) style. *For more information on how to cite your sources see Appendix C. In addition, consider the following:

1. How does the introduction engage the reader's attention?
2. What pieces of supporting evidence are used to back up the essay's points and arguments?
3. What purpose do the essay's quotes serve?
4. How does the author transition from one idea to another?

■ Refers to thesis and topic sentences

■ Refers to supporting details

Paragraph 1

Note how the introduction attempts to capture your imagination and attention. Do you find it to be an effective way of opening the essay?

Do you enjoy nature hiking through a dense forest, soaking up the sounds of croaking frogs and whistling birds? What about SCUBA diving in the open ocean, scouring the colorful reefs for schools of large fish, exotic turtles, and other

*Editor's Note: In applying MLA style guidelines in this book, the following simplifications have been made: Parenthetical text citations are confined to direct quotations only; electronic source documentation in the Works Cited list omits date of access, page ranges, and some detailed facts of publication.

creatures? These and other activities allow humans to get close to animals and plants of hundreds of different species. But are all of these species thriving? Not likely: in 2007 there were approximately 1,880 species listed as endangered, about 1,310 of which are found in the U.S. and its waters. To better understand what makes a species endangered, it is helpful to contrast a few important differences between healthy and endangered species.

This is the essay's thesis statement. It tells the reader what the essay will be about.

Paragraph 2

The biggest indicator of an endangered species is whether its habitat is threatened. Indeed, all species need intact habitats to survive. Habitats are complicated ecosystems comprised of space, water, food, animals, plants, insects, and weather. Changes to any of these factors impact a species' ability to survive. In the case of endangered species, much of their habitat has been lost, typically due to human activity such as agriculture, pollution, or deforestation. The orangutan, for example, has lost much of its habitat to deforestation by humans. The forests in which the orangutan lives have been cleared or burned to make room for agriculture fields and business endeavors such as oil palm plantations. For these reasons, the orangutan has been listed as endangered since 2000. According to the IUCN (World Conservation Union) 2006 Red List, which annually evaluates the status of all endangered and threatened species, the orangutan is believed to have suffered a 50 percent population loss since 1999. "It is projected that this trend will continue given the current circumstances," concluded the report at its time of assessment. (Euday) The habitats of non-endangered species, on the other hand, remain able to sustain healthy populations. Whether a species' habitat is threatened or not is key to its status as endangered.

The highlighted words all serve as transitional phrases that help the author flow from one idea to another.

"On the other hand" indicates a comparison is being made.

Paragraph 3

This is the topic sentence of paragraph 3. It lets the reader know this paragraph will focus on contrasting differences in exploitation of healthy and endangered species.

Another difference between endangered species and other species is whether it is prone to exploitation, that is, over-hunting or overfishing. Some species, such as salmon, are raised in fish farms to prevent overfishing the ocean's natural schools. Other species, such as deer, are so abundant that during some seasons sport hunters are actually encouraged to kill them to help keep their numbers down. But some are hunted to the brink of extinction. Whales, for example, prized for their blubber and oil, were so over hunted in the 19th century it was expected they would be driven to extinction by the end of the 20th century. Other species have been exploited because of medicinal properties their body parts are believed to have. For instance, Philippine fruit bats have been hunted nearly out of existence for their aphrodisiac properties. For these reasons, writer J.D. Smith has proposed that introducing pharmaceuticals that do the same job as endangered species parts could help save many types of animals and plants. Writes Smith, "If we want to save black bears and rhinos, we have to get these drugs into the hands of the people who would otherwise be paying for those animals' parts. ... [This] could be one of the most important conservation initiatives of our time."

This quote was taken from Viewpoint 6. How does it support the author's point in paragraph 3?

Paragraph 4

This is the topic sentence of paragraph 4. It indicates a new idea is being introduced.

A third difference between endangered and non-endangered species is whether they are affected by what is known as an "invasive" species; that is, a species not natural to a habitat or climate. Invasive species are usually introduced to a habitat by human activity, and tend to be highly adaptable. One devastating invasive species is the brown tree snake, which, during World War II, hitched a ride aboard a ship that sailed to the island of Guam. With no natural predators, the snake reproduced quickly and killed almost the entire native bird population on the previously snake-free island. Today the brown tree snake threatens to decimate the bird populations of the Hawaiian Islands as it did to those on

The author has offered two specific examples of invasive species to make her point. Always support your ideas with specific, rather than general, pieces of evidence.

Guam. In another example, the invasive plant species purple loosestrife has dramatically changed the ecology of certain wetlands by reducing the abundance of native plants. This in turn has reduced the food supply of ducks and turtles, both of which have become endangered. According to a 2005 study on invasive species published in *Ecological Economics,* an estimated 80 percent of endangered species around the world could suffer losses due to competition with or predation by invasive species.

Referencing authoritative sources helps lend your essay legitimacy.

Disappearing habitat, over-hunting, and invasive species are just three threats that render a species endangered. Overcoming these losses will be key to saving endangered species from becoming extinct, and preventing scores of other species from being classified as endangered. Differentiating between healthy and endangered species brings us one step closer to protecting all species and protecting the Earth's beauty and diversity.

Note how the conclusion touches on what has been covered without simply restating points made earlier in the essay.

Works Cited

Eudey, A. & Members of the Primate Specialist Group 2000. *Pongo abelii.* In: IUCN 2006. *2006 IUCN Red List of Threatened Species.* www.iucnredlist.org. Accessed April 15, 2007.

Smith, J.D. "An Immodest Proposal." *Grist* 22 Mar. 2005.

Exercise 1A: Create an Outline from an Existing Essay

It often helps to create an outline of the five-paragraph essay before you write it. The outline can help you organize the information, arguments, and evidence you have gathered during your research.

For this exercise, create an outline that could have been used to write "What Makes a Species Endangered?" This "reverse engineering" exercise is meant to help familiarize you with how outlines can help classify and arrange information.

To do this you will need to
1. articulate the essay's thesis;
2. pinpoint important pieces of evidence;
3. flag quotes that supported the essay's ideas; and
4. identify key points that supported the argument.

Part of the outline has already been started to give you an idea of the assignment.

Outline

I. **Paragraph One**

A. Write the essay's thesis or main objective: To analyze the differences between healthy and endangered species.

II. **Paragraph Two**

Topic: Whether a species' habitat is threatened or not is key to its status as endangered.

A.

B. Statistic and quote from the IUCN Red List

III. Paragraph Three

Topic:

A. Some species, such as deer, are intentionally hunted to keep their numbers down.

B. Other species, such as Philippine fruit bats, are hunted to near extinction for their medicinal properties.

IV. Paragraph Four

Topic:

A. The brown tree snake decimated bird populations in Guam and threatens to do the same thing in the Hawaiian Islands.

B.

V. Paragraph Five

A. Write the essay's conclusion:

Choosing Owls over Humans

Refers to thesis and topic sentences

Refers to supporting details

Editor's Notes The second essay, also written in five paragraphs, is a slightly different type of compare-and-contrast essay than the first model essay. In the first essay, the author contrasted the differences between two subjects without expressing a perspective or opinion. In the following essay, the author compares two subjects and expresses a preference for one side over another. This is called a persuasive or opinionated essay, and is meant to convince the reader to agree with the author's point of view.

The notes in the sidebars provide questions that will help you analyze how this essay is organized and how it is written.

Paragraph 1

Humans must coexist with the environment. But what happens when the rights of animals trump the rights of humans? A sad example of this occurred in the early 1990s when efforts to protect the Northern Spotted Owl in the Pacific Northwest resulted in the loss of thousands of logging jobs, leading to a devastating economic downturn in the region. Animals deserve to be protected, and endangered species even more so. But when such protection comes at the expense of whole communities, we must question the wisdom of environmental policies that choose animals over humans.

What is the essay's thesis statement? How do you know this will be a persuasive essay?

Paragraph 2

On the one hand, the endangerment of the Northern Spotted Owl is a sad comment on the plight of endangered species in the U.S. Of the approximately 1880 species listed as endangered, more than 1300 of them reside in the U.S. In 1990, the Northern Spotted Owl became one of these. By the early 1990s the owl population's habitat in Northern California,

"On the one hand" is a transitional phrase that lets the reader know a comparison will be made. What other transitions are in the essay?

Oregon, and Washington had been so devastated that there were only about three to five thousand pairs remaining in the wild, while the Canadian population numbers less than 20 birds. To protect the birds, a 1991 court order halted all logging in the region, a move that was hailed by environmentalists. But even these efforts may have been too late to save the owls; in 2001, several studies determined the owls were still declining at about 6 percent per year, which could mean their extinction by 2017. Environmentalists such as Sybil Ackerman of the Portland, Oregon Audubon Society have opposed plans to reinstate logging in the region, trying at all costs to prevent the extinction of the owl. Said Ackerman: "We've already logged it [the old-growth forests the owls need for habitat] like crazy. All we're asking is to save some of it for owls. We don't need this (timber) windfall at the expense of the species." (qtd. in Spark)

Paragraph 2 lays out one side of the spotted owl controversy. These ideas will be compared with a different perspective in the following paragraphs.

What does the Ackerman quote add to paragraph 2? What qualifies this person to speak on this topic?

Paragraph 3

While the near-extinction of the owl and the lost of old-growth forests is sad, it is not nearly as disturbing as the effect the 1991 ban on old-growth forest logging had on the Pacific Northwest. The ban resulted in the closing of nearly 1,000 sawmills and pulp and paper mills, and in the loss of more than 130,000 jobs. These job losses decimated already struggling families, many of whom were forced to move from their homes. Area schools and business were forced into closure due to the economic decline of the region. Harvests of timber in the Pacific Northwest were reduced by 80 percent, decreasing the supply of lumber and increasing prices all over the nation. In fact, the *Wall Street Journal* reported a 25 percent cost increase in wood products. "Thus the nation, not just loggers, are impacted by the ESA listing of the spotted owl," writes T. R. Mader, research director of the Abundant Wildlife Society of North America, which opposes the logging ban. Bumper stickers reading *Kill a Spotted Owl—Save a Logger* pretty much summed up the local feeling that environmentalists had chosen animals over people.

How does this sentence help transition between paragraph 2 and 3?

What are some of the supporting details of paragraph 3?

Paragraph 4

There is debate surrounding the extent to which the logging ban caused the economic downturn in the Pacific Northwest. According to studies at the University of Madison, Wisconsin, and the University of Oregon, the timber industry was in decline anyway, and only about 9,000 jobs could be directly attributed to the owl controversy. But regardless of how many jobs were specifically lost, the controversy over the owl habitat raises the question of whether an animal's right to survival should trump a person's livelihood. While no one wants to see species be driven into extinction, no one wants to see families driven into poverty and whole communities decimated. Animals can only be helped to survive so much; at some point one must realize that if they are unable to adapt to new surroundings, their survival is questionable anyway. As Mader writes, "Extinction is a normal part of the natural evolutionary process. …Failure to recognize this phenomena will result in wasting expertise and money on recovery programs doomed to failure by this natural process while people lose their jobs and go hungry."

Paragraph 5

What is the topic sentence of the last paragraph?

The Northern Spotted Owl controversy is just one example of well-intentioned environmental policies that trample the rights of humans. The U.S. must strive to adopt environmental policies that protect endangered species yet also protect the livelihoods of American citizens. As commentator Rush Limbaugh argued during the spotted owl controversy, the protection of business is at times more important than the protection of nature. "If a spotted owl can't adapt, does the earth really need that particular species so much that hardship to human beings is worth enduring in the process of saving it? … There's no reason to put the timber business out of commission just because of 2,200 pairs of one kind of owl [at the expense of] 30,000 jobs. That's the wrong set

How does the writer avoid simply repeating the main ideas of the essay?

of priorities." Indeed, while protecting the environment is important, it should not take priority over the well-being of American citizens.

Works Cited

Limbaugh, Rush. "Priority on people, not on spotted owls." *The Way Things Ought To Be* 2 July 1992: 160–61.

Mader, T.R. "Endangered Species Act: Flawed Law." Abundant Wildlife Society of North America 11 March 2004. www. aws.vcn.com/flawed/html Accessed April 16, 2007.

Stark, Mike. "Will Logging Save the Spotted Owl?" *High Country News* 12 March 2001 http://www.hcn.org/serv-lets/hcn.Article?article_id = 1030 Accessed April 16, 2007.

Exercise 2A: Create an Outline from an Existing Essay

As you did for the first model essay in this section, create an outline that could have been used to write "Choosing Owls over Humans." Be sure to identify the essay's thesis statement, its supporting ideas, its descriptive passages, and key pieces of evidence that were used.

Exercise 2B: Create an Outline for Your Own Essay

The second model essay expresses a particular point of view about endangered species. For this exercise, your assignment is to find supporting ideas, choose specific and concrete details, create an outline, and ultimately write a five-paragraph essay making a different, or even opposing, point about endangered species. Your goal is to use compare-and-contrast techniques to convince your reader.

Step I: Write a thesis statement.

The following thesis statement would be appropriate for an opposing essay on why it is important to protect endangered species even at the expense of the economy:

Like spotted owls and other species, humans are dependant on the bounty of natural resources; without protection of habitat and endangered species, none of us would be able to survive.

Or, see the sample paper topics suggested in Appendix D for more ideas.

Step II: Brainstorm pieces of supporting evidence.

Using information from some of the viewpoints in the previous section and from the information found in Section III of this book, write down three arguments or pieces of evidence that support the thesis statement you selected. Then, for each of these three arguments, write down supportive facts, examples, and details that support it. These could be:

- statistical information
- personal memories and anecdotes
- quotes from experts, peers, or family members
- observations of people's actions and behaviors
- specific and concrete details

Supporting pieces of evidence for the above sample topic sentence are found in this book and include:

- Point from Viewpoint 4 arguing that protection of the southern sea otter has resulted in increased tourism to California, providing local economies with valuable income.
- Quote box in Viewpoint 1 from British Ecological Society science policy manager Nick Dusic arguing that caring for the environment is critical to our own survival: "The services that ecosystems provide are fundamental to our well-being. ... When we over-exploit fish stocks, our economy grows more slowly than it otherwise would, due to the loss of the fishing industry. When we log upland forests, we are less secure due to the increased risk of flooding. When we pollute freshwater ecosystems, we are less healthy due to poor water quality."

Step III: Place the information from Step I in outline form.

Step IV: Write the arguments or supporting statements in paragraph form.

By now you have three arguments that support the paragraph's thesis statement, as well as supporting material. Use the outline to write out your three supporting arguments in paragraph form. Make sure each paragraph has a topic sentence that states the paragraph's thesis clearly and broadly. Then add supporting sentences that express the facts, quotes, details, and examples that support the paragraph's argument. The paragraph may also have a concluding or summary sentence.

Cloning or Habitat Preservation? The Race to Save Endangered Species

Editor's Notes The final model essay compares and contrasts what cloning and habitat preservation can offer the fight to save endangered species. It lays out the benefits and drawbacks of each and concludes that the two methods will best protect endangered species by being used in conjunction with each other.

This essay differs from the previous model essays in that it is longer than five paragraphs. Sometimes five paragraphs are simply not enough to adequately develop an idea. Extending the length of an essay can allow the writer to explore a topic in more depth or present multiple pieces of evidence that together provide a complete picture of a topic. Longer essays can also help writers discover the complexity of a subject by examining a topic beyond its superficial exterior. Moreover, the ability to write a sustained research or position paper is a valuable skill you will need as you advance academically.

As you read, consider the questions posed in the margins. Continue to identify thesis statements, supporting details, transitions, and quotations. Examine the introductory and concluding paragraphs to understand how they give shape to the essay. Finally, evaluate the essay's general structure and assess its overall effectiveness.

███ Refers to thesis and topic sentences

███ Refers to supporting details

Paragraph 1

Species extinction is one of the most rapidly growing environmental problems the earth faces in the 21st century. According to the World Conservation Union, humans have caused species to become extinct at a rate 100 to 11,000 times faster than natural extinction rates. As scientists, politicians, and other leaders search for answers to this

What problem is established in the introductory paragraph?

problem, cloning has been suggested as a way to preserve endangered species and regenerate extinct ones. Indeed, "frozen zoos" containing biological samples from extinct and endangered animals have popped up in government laboratories, universities, and the stocks of private companies. Yet some believe a better way to prevent species extinction is to preserve habitat, the loss of which is the number one cause of species extinction. It is useful to compare and contrast habitat preservation with cloning to determine which can better rectify damage done to the Earth's endangered and extinct plants and animals.

What is the essay's thesis statement?

Paragraph 2

Advocates of cloning say it can help save endangered species by artificially adding numbers to a species' population, helping it survive despite exploitation (such as over-hunting or overfishing) or habitat loss. This was the driving force behind the successful cloning in 2003 of an endangered African wildcat, whose numbers are dramatically low. Efforts have also been made to clone the guar, an endangered wild ox found in Asia, the bucardo, an extinct Spanish mountain goat, as well as the giant panda, the African bongo antelope, the Sumatran tiger, the cheetah, and other endangered species. George Amato, director of the Science Resource Center at the Wildlife Conservation Society in New York, gives the example of "the Sumatran rhino, of which there are only 15 breeding pairs in captivity and maybe a few hundred in the wild" to explain why society must be open to technologies that allow species to increase their numbers. (qtd. in Quick)

Make a list of experts quoted in this essay, noting what qualifies them to speak on this topic.

What is the topic sentence of paragraph 2?

Paragraph 3

Cloning can also help enlarge the genetic diversity of small animal populations, which can prevent a dwindling population from inbreeding and suffering birth defects and other species-threatening health problems. When a species is threatened and its population decreases, its genetic pool

What is the topic sentence of paragraph 3?

becomes more limited (because there are fewer animals available to reproduce). When animals have fewer companions to mate with, they tend to inbreed, which causes the development of genetic diseases that render the species prone to birth defects and other health problems. But if healthy, strong, and genetically diverse animals are cloned, it could help eliminate disease among a population, further protecting it from dying out. Writes the Audubon Nature Institute, a proponent of cloning to save endangered species, "Cloning of healthy animals can be introduced into wild populations and give a 'booster shot' of fresh genetic material to a species undergoing a lost genetic diversity."

This quote was taken from Viewpoint 5. Remember to retain useful quotes to support points you make in your papers.

Paragraph 4

Because of these benefits, many scientists view cloning as an invaluable tool in the fight against species extinction. Says Dr. Betsy L. Dresser, who has participated in endangered species cloning projects at the Audubon Nature Institute, "Technology alone will not be enough to save endangered species, but it's impossible to win the battle against extinction without it. Now we have new tools we can use to keep hope alive for species facing dramatically dwindling numbers." (qtd. in "Nuclear Transfer (Cloning)")

Paragraph 5

On the other hand, many argue that cloning to save endangered species (and cloning efforts in general) constitutes an immoral use of science. Indeed, cloning and other types of genetic engineering are often criticized for letting humans irresponsibly play God. It goes against the natural order to artificially resurrect species that became extinct decades, even hundreds of years, ago. For these reasons many people, such as reporter Sylvia Pagan Westphal, view efforts to clone endangered species as immoral: "Although cloning could help us conserve endangered species, it cannot salve humanity's conscience by raising the dead. Extinction is still forever." (40)

What transitional phrases are used that let you know a comparison is being made?

How does the Westphal quote directly support the point made before it?

Paragraph 6

Another strike against cloning is the fact that the technology is still very new and unreliable. In addition to being expensive, many cloned endangered species do not survive long enough to help their population. For example, in January 2001, the company Advanced Cell Technology (ACT) successfully cloned a guar, yet it died two days later. Furthermore, ACT's efforts to clone a bucardo have been stalled since 2002. Finally, saving endangered species is not as clear-cut as simply regenerating a few animals. Species do not exist in a vacuum; they need an entire ecosystem, built of habitat and other species, to survive. As one author writes, "With countless species going extinct, replacing every creature in an ecosystem probably would be impossible. To fully reconstruct a habitat would mean not only recreating monkeys, wolves and birds, but also beetles, flies and frogs." (Hembree 2)

What specific facts and examples are used to reinforce claims made by the author?

Paragraph 7

Opponents of cloning endangered species claim it is a superficial fix to an extensive, multifaceted problem. Simply mass-producing endangered species, it is argued, deemphasizes the importance of protecting habitat and preventing the exploitation of natural resources, two of the primary reasons species are endangered in the first place. "I'm not saying that cloning endangered species is a bad thing, or that people are giving up work in other areas of nature conservation because of it," writes one observer. "But I'm afraid that it gives many, like with hydrogen fuel cell technology, the false impression that a solution is coming." ("Cloning Endangered Species—Watch Out!") Indeed, cloning endangered species does nothing to attack the root of the endangered species problem, and for this reason seems to be a misleading panacea to what is a serious environmental problem facing the Earth and all its inhabitants.

The author uses paragraphs 7 and 8 to analyze claims set down in preceding paragraphs.

It is usually inappropriate to use the first person, or "I", when writing a formal essay. Therefore, use quotes to express a more personal position for you.

Paragraph 8

Preserving habitat, on the other hand, is an effort that fundamentally attacks the root of the endangered species problem. Writes one analyst for the non-profit environmental group CETOS: "We are at a juncture where we can … selflessly begin to curb the very activities that are decimating animals in the wild. Instead of the millions being spent to clone a single member of a complex web of animals in danger of extinction, why not restore their habitat?" Because habitat desecration is the number one cause of species extinction, it seems the most critical problem to address in the fight to save endangered animals.

What is the topic sentence of paragraph 8?

Paragraph 9

But the preservation of habitat is an extremely complex and challenging undertaking. Preventing habitat destruction often conflicts with the interests of business. The main reason why habitats such as the rainforests are lost is because of over-farming or slash-and-burn agricultural techniques used to feed developing populations; or over-collection of a natural resource that erodes the delicate ecosystem but provides ingredients for valuable products, such as medicines. Indeed, according to the National Wildlife Federation's Endangered Species Program, about 40 percent of all prescriptions are derived from the natural compounds of different species. These species not only save lives, but contribute to a prospering pharmaceutical industry worth over $40 billion annually. When preserving habitat for endangered species means cutting into profits, it will not be an easy fight to win.

The author devotes paragraph 9 to discussing the obstacles of preserving habitat as a way to save endangered species.

Paragraph 10

Neither cloning nor habitat preservation are silver bullets for preventing species extinction. Cloning, or any other technology, should not be used as a substitute for treating the Earth responsibly. Humans must recognize and prevent the

What is the topic sentence of paragraph 10? How is it critical to the essay as a whole?

practices that led to the endangerment and extinction of so many species in the first place. Preserving habitat is key to this endeavor. If humanity does not learn to preserve habitat, there is nothing to prevent cloned endangered species from succumbing to lost habitat and becoming over-hunted, just like their natural predecessors.

Paragraph 11

In contrast, pro-cloning activists such as Audubon Nature Institute's Center for Research of Endangered Species spokeswoman Sarah Burnette, rightly point out that it could take so long to adequately preserve habitat that by the time business interests are reconciled with environmental ones, there may be no animals left to protect at all. Asks Burnette, "What if 100 years from now people finally figure out how to save the habitats, but there are no animals?" For this Burnette logically concludes, "(Cloning) is part of the answer." (qtd. in Humbree 2)

Paragraph 12

How does the conclusion return to the task laid out in the introductory paragraph? Did the essay accomplish what it set out to?

After comparing cloning and habitat preservation, it seems clear that the two efforts should be pursued concurrently to prevent species extinction. Indeed, the race to prevent species extinction should be a multi-pronged effort focusing on different fronts. Until cloning becomes more reliable, less expensive, and more socially acceptable, habitat preservation should be pursued. Conversely, if efforts to save habitat continue to be trumped by business interests, cloning should be relied upon to preserve species until habitat can be set aside for them.

Works Cited

Bailey, Britt. "Cloning the Guar." Center for Ethics & Toxics. http://www.cetos.org/articles/cloninggaur.html. Accessed April 15, 2007.

"Cloning Endangered Species—Watch Out!" *Treehugger.com* 25 May 2005. http://www.treehugger.com/files/2005/05/cloning_endange_1.php. Accessed April 12, 2007.

Hembree, Amy. "Cloning Is No Extinction Panacea." *Wired* 13 Feb. 2001: 2. http://www.wired.com/science/discoveries/news/2001/02/41704?currentPage = 1. Accessed April 12, 2007.

"Nuclear Transfer (Cloning)." Audubon Nature Institute, 2006.

Quick, Susanne. "Conservationists Debate Cloning Rare Species." *Milwaukee Journal Sentinel* 29 Mar. 2005.

Westphal, Sylvia Pagan. "Copy and Save." *New Scientist* 19 June 2004: 36–40.

Exercise 3A: Examining Introductions and Conclusions

Every essay features introductory and concluding paragraphs that are used to frame the main ideas being presented. Along with presenting the essay's thesis statement, well-written introductions should grab the attention of the reader and make clear why the topic being explored is important. The conclusion reiterates the essay's thesis and is also the last chance for the writer to make an impression on the reader. Strong introductions and conclusions can greatly enhance an essay's effect on an audience.

The Introduction

There are several techniques that can be used to craft an introductory paragraph. An essay can start with:

- an anecdote: a brief story that illustrates a point relevant to the topic;
- startling information: facts or statistics that elucidate the point of the essay;
- setting up and knocking down a position: a position or claim believed by proponents of one side of a controversy, followed by statements that challenge that claim;
- historical perspective: an example of the way things used to be that leads into a discussion of how or why things work differently now;
- summary information: general introductory information about the topic that feeds into the essay's thesis statement.

Problem One
Reread the introductory paragraphs of the model essays and of the viewpoints in Section I. Identify which of the techniques described above are used in the example essays. How do they grab the attention of the reader? Are their thesis statements clearly presented?

Problem Two
Write an introduction for the essay you have outlined and partially written in Exercise 2B using one of the techniques described above.

The Conclusion

The conclusion brings the essay to a close by summarizing or returning to its main ideas. Good conclusions, however, go beyond simply repeating these ideas. Strong conclusions explore a topic's broader implications and reiterate why it is important to consider. They may frame the essay by returning to an anecdote featured in the opening paragraph. Or, they may close with a quotation or refer back to an event in the essay. In opinionated essays, the conclusion can reiterate which side the essay is taking or ask the reader to reconsider a previously held position on the subject.

Problem One
Reread the concluding paragraphs of the model essays and of the viewpoints in Section I. Which were most effective in driving their arguments home to the reader? What sorts of techniques did they use to do this? Did they appeal emotionally to the reader, or bookend an idea or event referenced elsewhere in the essay?

Problem Two
Write a conclusion for the essay you have outlined and partially written in Exercise 2B using one of the techniques described above.

Exercise 3B: Using Quotations to Enliven Your Essay

No essay is complete without quotations. Get in the habit of using quotes to support at least some of the ideas in your essays. Quotes do not need to appear in every paragraph, but often enough so that the essay contains voices aside from your own. When you write, use quotations to accomplish the following:

- Provide expert advice that you are not necessarily in the position to know about.
- Cite lively or passionate passages.
- Include a particularly well-written point that gets to the heart of the matter.
- Supply statistics or facts that have been derived from someone's research.
- Deliver anecdotes that illustrate the point you are trying to make.
- Express first-person testimony.

There are a couple of important things to remember when using quotations.

- Note your sources' qualifications and biases. This way your reader can identify the person you have quoted and can put their words in a context.
- Put any quoted material within proper quotation marks. Failing to attribute quotes to their authors constitutes plagiarism, which is when an author takes someone else's words or ideas and presents them as their own. Plagiarism is a very serious infraction and must be avoided at all costs.

Problem One: Reread the essays presented in all sections of this book and find at least one example of each of the above quotation types.

Write Your Own Compare-And-Contrast Five-Paragraph Essay

Using the information from this book, write your own five-paragraph compare-and-contrast essay that deals with endangered species. You can use the sources in this book for information about issues relating to this topic and how to structure this type of essay. The following steps are suggestions on how to get started.

Step One: Choose your topic.
The first step is to decide what topic to write your compare-and-contrast essay on. Is there any subject that particularly fascinates you? Is there an issue you strongly support, or feel strongly against? Is there a topic you feel personally connected to or one that you would like to learn more about? Ask yourself such questions before selecting your essay topic. Refer to Appendix D: Sample Essay Topics if you need help selecting a topic.

Step Two: Write down questions and answers about the topic.
Before you begin writing, you will need to think carefully about what ideas your essay will contain. This is a process known as *brainstorming*. Brainstorming involves asking yourself questions and coming up with ideas to discuss in your essay. Possible questions that will help you with the brainstorming process include:

- Why is this topic important?
- Why should people be interested in this topic?
- How can I make this essay interesting to the reader?
- What question am I going to address in this paragraph or essay?

- What facts, ideas, or quotes can I use to support the answer to my question?

Questions especially for compare-and-contrast essays include:

- Have I chosen subjects that I can compare or contrast?
- What characteristics do my subjects share?
- What is different about my subjects?
- Is one subject consistently superior to another?
- Is one subject consistently inferior to another?

Step Three: Gather facts, ideas, and anecdotes related to your topic.

This book contains several places to find information, including the viewpoints and the appendices. In addition, you may want to research the books, articles, and Web sites listed in Section III, or do additional research in your local library. You can also conduct interviews if you know someone who has a compelling story that would fit well in your essay.

Step Four: Develop a workable thesis statement.

Use what you have written down in steps two and three to help you articulate the main point or argument you want to make in your essay. It should be expressed in a clear sentence and make an arguable or supportable point.

Example:

We need malls, offices, and housing developments more than we need nesting grounds for condors. (This could be the thesis statement of a compare-and-contrast essay that compares the benefits of industry with the benefits of habitat conservation and concludes that society benefits more from development than protecting endangered species.)

Step Five: Write an outline or diagram.

1. Write the thesis statement at the top of the outline.
2. Write roman numerals I, II, and III on the left side of the page.
3. Next to each roman numeral, write down the best ideas you came up with in step three. These should all directly relate to and support the thesis statement. If the essay is solely a compare or solely a contrast essay, write down three similarities or three differences between your subjects. If it is a persuasive compare-and-contrast essay, write down three reasons why one subject or argument is superior to the other
4. Next to each letter write down information that supports that particular idea.

An alternative to the roman numeral outline is a diagram.

Diagrams: Alternative to Outlines

Some students might prefer to organize their ideas without using the roman numeral outline. One way to do this is to use the diagram method. Compare-and-contrast essays are especially well suited for the diagram method, which allows you to physically visualize the similarities and differences between your subjects. A possible approach would be as follows:

1. Draw two intersecting circles in the middle of a page so that one side of each overlaps.
2. On the left side of the page above the first circle, write "Subject A." In this circle, write all of the things that are unique to one subject.
3. On the right side of the page above the second circle, write "Subject B." Use this circle to jot down all of the things that are unique to the other subject.

4. In the middle of the page, above where the two circles intersect, write "A and B." In this intersected space, write all of the things that are common to both subjects.

Step Six: Write the three supporting paragraphs.

Use your outline to write the three supporting paragraphs. Write down the main idea of each paragraph in sentence form. Do the same thing for the supporting points of information. Each sentence should support the paragraph of the topic. Be sure you have relevant and interesting details, facts, and quotes. Use transitions when you move from idea to idea to keep the text fluid and smooth. Sometimes, although not always, paragraphs can include a concluding or summary sentence that restates the paragraph's argument.

Step Seven: Write the introduction and conclusion.

See Exercise 3B for information on writing introductions and conclusions.

Step Eight: Read and rewrite.

As you read, check your essay for the following:

✔ Does the essay maintain a consistent tone?

✔ Do all paragraphs reinforce your general thesis?

✔ Do all paragraphs flow from one to the other? Do you need to add transition words or phrases?

✔ Have you quoted from reliable, authoritative, and interesting sources?

✔ Is there a sense of progression throughout the essay?

✔ Does the essay get bogged down in too much detail or irrelevant material?

✔ Does your introduction grab the reader's attention?

✔ Does your conclusion reflect back on any previously discussed material or give the essay a sense of closure?

✔ Are there any spelling or grammatical errors?

Section Three: Supporting Research Material

Facts About Endangered Species

Extinction

Although the extinction of various species is a natural phe-nomenon, the rate of extinction occurring in today's world is exceptional—estimates range from one hundred to one thousand times greater than normal.

According to a report by the Center for Biological Diversity, 108 animals and plants have become extinct in the U.S. since the creation of the Endangered Species Act in 1973.

According to the U.S. Fish and Wildlife Service, losing one plant species can trigger the loss of up to 30 other insect, plant and higher animal species.

Endangered and Threatened Species

The 2006 IUCNs (World Conservation Union) Red List of Threatened Species listed the following as endangered or threatened:

    1093 species of mammals
    1206 species of birds
    341 species of reptiles
    1811 species of amphibians
    1173 species of fishes
    5624 total animal species

    623 species of insects
    975 species of molluscs
    459 species of crustaceans
    2101 total invertebrate species

    80 species of mosses
    139 species of ferns
    8390 total species of plants
    2 species of lichens
    1 species of mushroom

For a total of 16,118 endangered or threatened species worldwide.

Threatened species include one in three amphibians, half of freshwater turtles, one in eight birds, and one in four mammals.

500 North American species have gone extinct in the last 400 years.

38 million acres of tropical rainforests are destroyed each year. Up to one half of the world's species live in these areas.

In 2006 the U.S., had 1178 mammals, plants, invertebrates, reptiles, amphibians, mollusks, and other species listed as threatened or endangered. These include:

- Grizzly bears
- Black bears
- 9 kinds of bats
- Caribou
- 5 kinds of fox
- 5 kinds of rat
- Otters
- Seals
- Sea Lions
- 7 kinds of whale
- 2 kinds of wolf

Some 20 percent of all bird species are under threat of extinction.

There are more than 3,500 protected areas in existence worldwide. These areas include parks, wildlife refuges and other reserves. They cover a total of nearly 2 million square miles (5 million square km), or 3 percent of our total land area.

One third of the United States' fish species, two-thirds of its crayfish species, and almost three-quarters of its mussel species are threatened.

According to the U.S. Fish and Wildlife Service, every American state has some species listed as endangered or threatened:

- Alabama—117 listings
- Alaska—13 listings
- Arizona—55 listings
- Arkansas—31 listings
- California—309 listings
- Colorado—32 listings
- Connecticut—22 listings
- Delaware—23 listings
- District of Columbia—8 listings
- Florida—112 listings
- Georgia—71 listings
- Hawaii—329 listings
- Idaho—24 listings
- Illinois —38 listings
- Indiana—32 listings
- Iowa—20 listings
- Kansas—17 listings
- Kentucky—42 listings
- Louisiana—30 listings
- Maine—17 listings
- Maryland—31 listings
- Massachusetts—28 listings
- Michigan—25 listings
- Minnesota—16 listings
- Mississippi—42 listings
- Missouri—31 listings
- Montana—15 listings
- Nebraska—18 listings
- Nevada—38 listings
- New Hampshire—15 listings
- New Jersey—27 listings
- New Mexico—46 listings
- New York—34 listings

- North Carolina—63 listings
- North Dakota—9 listings
- Ohio—30 listings
- Oklahoma—20 listings
- Oregon—57 listings
- Pennsylvania—25 listings
- Rhode Island—19 listings
- South Carolina—42 listings
- South Dakota—12 listings
- Tennessee—90 listings
- Texas—94 listings
- Utah—43 listings
- Vermont—12 listings
- Virginia—66 listings
- Washington—43 listings
- West Virginia—23 listings
- Wisconsin—19 listings
- Wyoming—16 listings
- American Samoa—4 listings
- Guam—13 listings
- Northern Mariana Islands—11 listings
- Puerto Rico—75 listings
- Virgin Islands—13 listings
- Outlying Caribbean Islands—0 listings
- Outlying Pacific Islands—3 listings

Since being listed as endangered or threatened, twenty species—including the American alligator, the Columbian white-tailed deer, the American peregrine falcon, the Arctic peregrine falcon, the Aleutian Canada goose, the brown pelican, the gray wolf, and the gray whale—have recovered their populations to non-endangered levels.

Endangered Species Protection Laws

Several laws have been adopted to protect and preserve endangered species and their habitat. The following summaries were taken from the U.S. Fish & Wildlife Service, Division of Law Enforcement.

Bald and Golden Eagle Protection Act (16 U.S.C. 668–668C).
Makes it illegal to import, export, or take bald or golden eagles, or to sell, purchase, or barter their parts, or products made from them, including their nests or eggs.

Migratory Bird Treaty Act (16 U.S.C. 703–712).
Makes it unlawful to pursue, hunt, kill, capture, possess, buy, sell, purchase, or barter any migratory bird, including the feathers or other parts, nests, eggs, or migratory bird products.

Lacey Act (18 U.S.C. 42; 16 U.S.C. 3371–3378).
Provides authority to the Secretary of the Interior to designate injurious wildlife and ensure the humane treatment of wildlife shipped to the United States. Prohibits the importation, exportation, transportation, sale, or purchase of fish and wildlife taken or possessed in violation of State, Federal, Indian tribal, and foreign laws.

Marine Mammal Protection Act (16 U.S.C. 1361–1407).
Establishes a moratorium on the taking and importation of marine mammals, including parts and products, and outlines conservation of marine mammals, including the sea otter, walrus, polar bear, dugong, and manatee.

Airborne Hunting Act (16 U.S.C. 742j–1).
Section 13 of the Fish and Wildlife Act of 1956 is commonly referred to as the Airborne Hunting Act, or Shooting From Aircraft Act, and prohibits taking or harassing wildlife from aircraft, except when protecting wildlife, livestock, and human health or safety.

National Wildlife Refuge System Administration Act of 1966 (16 U.S.C. 668dd–668ee).
Provides guidelines and directives for administration and management of all areas in the system including "wildlife refuges, areas for the protection and conservation of fish and wildlife that are threatened with extinction, wildlife ranges, game ranges, wildlife management areas, or waterfowl production areas."

Endangered Species Act (16 U.S.C. 1531–1543).
Prohibits the importation, exportation, taking, and commercialization in interstate or foreign commerce of fish and wildlife, and plants that are listed as threatened or endangered species.

Antarctic Conservation Act (16 U.S.C. 2401).
Provides for the conservation and protection of the fauna and flora of Antarctica and of the ecosystem upon which such fauna and flora depend. Makes it unlawful for any United States citizen to take any native bird or mammal in Antarctica or to collect any native plant from any specially protected area within Antarctica. In addition, the Act makes it unlawful for any United States citizen or any foreign person in the United States to possess, sell, offer for sale, deliver, receive, carry, transport, import, export, or attempt to import or export from the United States any native mammal or bird taken in Antarctica or any plant collected in any specially protected area.

African Elephant Conservation Act (16 U.S.C. 4201–4245).
Provides protection for the African elephant. Establishes an assistance program to elephant producing countries of Africa and provides for the establishment of an African Elephant Conservation Fund. In addition, the Act places a moratorium on the importation of raw or worked ivory from African-elephant-producing countries that do not meet certain criteria found in the Act.

Wild Bird Conservation Act of 1992 (16 U.S.C. 4901).
Promotes the conservation of exotic birds by encouraging wild bird conservation and management programs in countries of origin; by ensuring that all trade in such species involving the United States is biologically sustainable and to the benefit of the species; and by limiting or prohibiting imports of exotic birds when necessary to ensure that exotic wild populations are not harmed by removal for the trade.

Finding and Using Sources of Information

No matter what type of essay you are writing, it is necessary to find information to support your point of view. You can use sources such as books, magazine articles, newspaper articles, and online articles.

Using Books and Articles

You can find books and articles in a library by using the library's computer or cataloging system. If you are not sure how to use these resources, ask a librarian to help you. You can also use a computer to find many magazine articles and other articles written specifically for the Internet.

You are likely to find a lot more information than you can possibly use in your essay, so your first task is to narrow it down to what is likely to be most usable. Look at book and article titles. Look at book chapter titles, and examine the book's index to see if it contains information on the specific topic you want to write about. (For example, if you want to write about over-fishing problems and you find a book about sharks, check the chapter titles and index to be sure it contains information about the exploitation of sharks before you bother to check out the book.)

For a five–paragraph essay, you do not need a great deal of supporting information, so quickly try to narrow down your materials to a few good books and magazine or Internet articles. You do not need dozens. You might even find that one or two good books or articles contain all the information you need.

You probably do not have time to read an entire book, so find the chapters or sections that relate to your topic, and skim these. When you find useful information, copy it onto a note card or notebook. You should look for supporting facts, statistics, quotations, and examples.

Using the Internet

When you select your supporting information, it is important that you evaluate its source. This is especially important with information you find on the Internet. Because nearly anyone can put information on the Internet, there is as much bad information as good information. Before using Internet information—or any information—try to determine if the source seems to be reliable. Is the author or Internet site sponsored by a legitimate organization? Is it from a government source? Does the author have any special knowledge or training relating to the topic you are looking up? Does the article give any indication of where its information comes from?

Using Your Supporting Information

When you use supporting information from a book, article, interview or other source, there are three important things to remember:

1. *Make it clear whether you are using a direct quotation or a paraphrase.* If you copy information directly from your source, you are quoting it. You must put quotation marks around the information, and tell where the information comes from. If you put the information in your own words, you are paraphrasing it.

Here is an example of using a quotation:

> Author Bjørn Lomborg believes that the problem of species extinction is a natural phenomenon. "The common claim that we're going to lose anywhere from 25 to 50 percent of all species in our lifetimes is simply not true," he writes. "It's not backed up by the data that we have. We've always lost species." ("Crisis Interviews Bjørn Lomborg"). Therefore, Lomborg urges policymakers not to base environmental laws on panic.

Here is an example of a brief paraphrase of the same passage:

> Author Bjørn Lomborg believes that the problem of species extinction is a natural phenomenon. He challenges claims that the planet is going to lose 25 to 50 percent of its species, arguing that the planet has always lost species: that is part and parcel of the evolutionary process. Therefore, Lomborg urges policymakers not to base environmental laws on panic.

2. *Use the information fairly.* Be careful to use supporting information in the way the author intended it. For example, it is unfair to quote an author as saying, "The endangered sea turtle population has seen a boom in recent years," when he or she intended to say, "The endangered sea turtle population has seen a boom in recent years, but is still well below healthy numbers and thus is still classified as an endangered species." This is called taking information out of context. This is using supporting evidence unfairly.

3. *Give credit where credit is due.* Giving credit is known as citing. You must use citations when you use someone else's information, but not every piece of supporting information needs a citation.

   - If the supporting information is general knowledge—that is, it can be found in many sources—you do not have to cite your source.
   - If you directly quote a source, you must cite it.
   - If you paraphrase information from a specific source, you must cite it.

If you do not use citations where you should, you are *plagiarizing*—or stealing—someone else's work.

Citing Your Sources

There are a number of ways to cite your sources. Your teacher will probably want you to do it in one of three ways:

- Informal: As in the example in number 1 above, tell where you got the information as you present it in the text of your essay.
- Informal list: At the end of your essay, place an unnumbered list of all the sources you used. This tells the reader where, in general, your information came from.
- Formal: Use numbered footnotes. Footnotes are generally placed at the end of an article or essay, although they may be placed elsewhere depending on your teacher's requirements.

Works Cited

"Crisis Interviews Bjørn Lomborg." *Crisis Magazine* 1 Apr. 2004.

Using MLA Style to Create a Works Cited List

You will probably need to create a list of works cited for your paper. These include materials that you quoted from, relied heavily on, or consulted to write your paper. There are several different ways to structure these references. The following examples are based on Modern Language Association (MLA) style, one of the major citation styles used by writers.

Book Entries

For most book entries you will need the author's name, the book's title, where it was published, what company published it, and the year it was published. This information is usually found on the inside of the book. Variations on book entries include the following:

A Book by a Single Author
Guest, Emma. *Children of AIDS: Africa's Orphan Crisis*. London: Sterling, 2003.

Two or More Books by the Same Author
Friedman, Thomas L. *The World Is Flat: A Brief History of the Twentieth Century*. New York: Farrar, Straus and Giroux, 2005.
---. *From Beirut to Jerusalem*. New York: Doubleday, 1989.

A Book by Two or More Authors
Pojman, Louis P., and Jeffrey Reiman. *The Death Penalty: For and Against*. Lanham, MD: Rowman & Littlefield, 1998.

A Book with an Editor
> Friedman, Lauri S., ed. *At Issue: What Motivates Suicide Bombers?* San Diego, CA: Greenhaven, 2004.

Periodical and Newspaper Entries

Entries for sources found in periodicals and newspapers are cited a bit differently than books. For one, these sources usually have a title and a publication name. They also may have specific dates and page numbers. Unlike book entries, you do not need to list where newspapers or periodicals are published or what company publishes them.

An Article from a Periodical
> Snow, Keith Harmon. "State Terror in Ethiopia." *Z Magazine* June 2004: 33–35.

An Unsigned Article from a Periodical
> "Broadcast Decency Rules." *Issues & Controversies on File* 30 Apr. 2004.

An Article from a Newspaper
> Constantino, Rebecca. "Fostering Love, Respecting Race." *Los Angeles Times* 14 Dec. 2002: B17.

Internet Sources

To document a source you found online, try to provide as much information on it as possible, including the author's name, the title of the document, date of publication or of last revision, the URL, and your date of access.

A Web Source
> Shyovitz, David. "The History and Development of Yiddish." Jewish Virtual Library. 30 May 2005 < http://www.jewishvirtuallibrary.org/jsource/History/yiddish.html. > . Accessed April 15, 2007.

Your teacher will tell you exactly how information should be cited in your essay. Generally, the very least information needed is the original author's name and the name of the article or other publication.

Be sure you know exactly what information your teacher requires before you start looking for your supporting information so that you know what information to include with your notes.

Sample Essay Topics

The Endangered Species Act Is Successful

The Endangered Species Act Is a Failure

The Endangered Species Act Should Be Reformed

The Endangered Species Act Threatens the Economy

Legislation Can Save Endangered Species

Legislation Can Not Save Endangered Species

The Interests of Animals Should Not Trump the Interests of Humans

The Interests of Animals and Humans are One and the Same

Preserving Endangered Species Should Take Precedence over Property Rights

Property Rights Should Not Be Sacrificed to Save Endangered Species

Zoos Can Help Save Endangered Species

Zoos Cannot Help Save Endangered Species

Distributing Pharmaceuticals to Third World Nations Can Prevent Exploitation of

Endangered Species

Education Can Help Prevent Exploitation of Endangered Species

The Introduction of Non-Native Species Threatens the Extinction of Native Populations

The Introduction of Non-Native Species Is Survival of the Fittest

Captive Breeding Programs Are Effective

Captive Breeding Programs Are Ineffective

Limiting Hunting Will Preserve Endangered Species

Limiting Hunting Will Hurt the Economy

Preserving Biodiversity Is Important

Not All Species Need to Be Preserved

Cloning Can Save Endangered Species

Organizations to Contact

American Forest and Paper Association (AFPA)
1111 19th St. NW, Ste. 800, Washington, DC 20036 •
(202) 463-2700 • fax: (202) 463-2471 • e-mail: info@
afandpa.org • Web site: http://www.afandpa.org

AFPA is a national trade association of the forest, pulp,
paper, paperboard, and wood products industry. The
association publishes materials on timber supply and forest management as well as the *International Trade Report,*
a monthly newsletter that features articles on current
issues affecting forest products, industry, and international trade.

American Livestock Breeds Conservancy (ALBC)
PO Box 477, Pittsboro, NC 27312 • (919) 542-5704 •
fax: (919) 545-0022 • e-mail: albc@albc-usa.org • Web
site: http://www.albc-usa.org

ALBC works to prevent the extinction of rare breeds of
American livestock. The conservancy believes that conservation is necessary to protect the genetic range and
survival ability of these species. ALBC provides general
information about the importance of saving rare breeds
as well as specific guidelines for individuals interested in
raising rare breeds.

American Zoo and Aquarium Association (AZA)
8403 Colseville Rd., Ste. 710, Silver Spring, MD 20910 •
Web site: http://www.aza.org

AZA represents over 160 zoos and aquariums in North
America. The association provides information on captive
breeding of endangered species, conservation education,
natural history, and wildlife legislation. AZA publications
include the *Species Survival Plans* and the *Annual Report on
Conservation and Science.*

Atlantic Salmon Federation (ASF)

PO Box 807, Calais, ME 04619-0807 • (506) 529-1033 • fax: (506) 529-4438 • e-mail: asf@nbnet.nb.ca • Web site: http://www.asf.ca

ASF is an international non-profit organization which promotes the conservation and wise management of the wild Atlantic salmon and its environment. It publishes the *Atlantic Salmon Journal,* the world's oldest publication for the conservation-minded salmon angler.

Canadian Forestry Association (CFA)

185 Somerset St. W, Ste. 203, Ottawa, ON K2P 0J2 Canada • (866) 639-6711 • e-mail: info@canadian-forests.com • Web site: http://www.canadian-forests.com

CFA works for improved forest management that would satisfy the economic, social, and environmental demands on Canadian forests. The association explores conflicting perspectives on forestry-related topics in its biannual Forest Forum.

The Captive Animal Protection Society (CAPS)

PO Box 43, Dudley DY3 2YP, England • Phone/fax: 01384-456682 • e-mail: info@captiveanimals.org • Web site: www.captiveanimals.org

CAPS was established in 1957 and is recognized today as one of the United Kingdom's leading campaigning organizations on behalf of animals in circuses, zoos, and the entertainment industry. CAPS is opposed to using performing animals in circuses.

Conservation International (CI)

2011 Crystal Drive, Suite 500 Arlington, VA 22202 • (800) 429-5660 • e-mail: info@conservation.org • Web site: http://www.conservation.org

CI believes that the Earth's natural heritage must be maintained if future generations are to thrive spiritually, culturally, and economically. CI's mission is to conserve the Earth's living natural heritage, our global biodiversity, and to demonstrate that human societies are able to live harmoniously with nature.

Defenders of Wildlife

1130 17th Street, NW Washington, DC 20036 • 800-385-9712 • e-mail: info@defenders.org • Web site: http://www.defenders.org

Defenders of Wildlife is dedicated to the protection of all native wild animals and plants in their natural communities. The organization focuses on the accelerating rate of extinction of species and the associated loss of biodiversity, and habitat alteration and destruction. The organization publishes *Defenders* magazine.

Endangered Species Coalition (ESC)

PO Box 65195, Washington, D.C. 20035 • (202) 682-9400 • e-mail: esc@stopextinction.org • Web site: http://www.stopextinction.org

The coalition is composed of conservation, professional, and animal welfare groups that work to extend the Endangered Species Act and to ensure its enforcement. ESC encourages public activism through grassroots organizations, direct lobbying, and letter-writing and telephone campaigns. Its publications include the book *The Endangered Species Act: A Commitment Worth Keeping* and numerous articles, fact sheets, position papers, and bill summaries regarding the Endangered Species Act.

Foundation for Research on Economics and the Environment (FREE)

662 Ferguson Rd., Ste. 101F, Bozeman, MT 59718 • (406) 585-1776 • fax: (406) 585-3000 • e-mail: jbaden@free-eco.org • Web site:http://www.free-eco.org

FREE is a research and education foundation committed to freedom, environmental quality, and economic progress. The foundation works to reform environmental policy by using the principles of private property rights, the free market, and the rule of law. FREE publishes the quarterly newsletter *FREE Perspective on Economics and the Environment* and produces a biweekly syndicated op-ed column.

International Society of Tropical Foresters (ISTF)

5400 Grosvenor Lane, Bethesda, MD 20814 • (301) 897-8720 • fax: (301) 897-3690 • e-mail: webmaster@istf-bethesda.org • Web site: http://www.istf-bethesda.org/

ISTF is a nonprofit international organization that strives to develop and promote ecologically sound methods of managing and harvesting tropical forests. The society provides information and technical knowledge about the effect of deforestation on agriculture, forestry, and industry. It publishes the quarterly newsletter *ISTF News*.

National Wildlife Federation (NWF)

11100 Wildlife Center Drive, Reston, VA 20190 • 800-822-9919 • Web site: http://www.nwf.org

The federation encourages the intelligent management of our natural resources and promotes the appreciation of such resources. It operates Ranger Rick's Wildlife Camp and sponsors National Wildlife Week. It also has a large library of conservation-related publications, which include *Ranger Rick's Nature Magazine* and *National Wildlife Magazine*.

North American Wolf Association (NAWA)

23214 Tree Bright St., Spring, TX 77373 • (281) 821-4884 • Web site: http://www.nawa.org

NAWA is a nonprofit organization dedicated to wolf recovery, reintroduction, rescue, and preservation.

PERC

2048 Analysis Dr. Ste. A, Bozeman, MT 59718 • (406) 587-9591 • e-mail: perc@perc.org • Web site: http://www.perc.org

PERC is a research center that provides solutions to environmental problems based on free market principles and the importance of property rights. PERC publications include the quarterly newsletter PERC Report and papers in the PERC Policy Series dealing with environmental issues.

Rainforest Action Network (RAN)

221 Pine St., Ste. 500, San Francisco, CA 94104 • (415) 398-4404 • Fax: (415) 398-2732 • e-mail: rainforest@ran.org • Web site: http://www.ran.org

RAN works to preserve the world's rain forests and protect the rights of native forest-dwelling peoples. The network sponsors letter-writing campaigns, boycotts, and demonstrations in response to environmental concerns. It publishes miscellaneous fact sheets, the monthly *Action Alert Bulletin*, and the quarterly *World Rainforest Report*.

U.S. Fish and Wildlife Service

Office of Public Affairs, 1849 C St. NW, Washington, DC 20240 • (202) 208-5634 • Web site: http://www.fws.gov

The U.S. Fish and Wildlife Service is a network of regional offices, national wildlife refuges, research and development centers, national fish hatcheries, and wildlife law enforcement agencies. The service's primary goal is to conserve, protect, and enhance fish and wildlife and their habitats. It publishes an endangered species list as well as facts sheets, pamphlets, and information on the Endangered Species Act.

World Wildlife Fund (WWF)
1250 24th St., NW, PO Box 97180, Washington, DC 20077-7180 • (800) 225-5993 • Web site: http://www.worldwildlife.org

WWF works to save endangered species, to conduct wildlife research, and to improve the natural environment. It publishes an endangered species list, the bimonthly newsletter *Focus,* and a variety of books on the environment.

Bibliography

Books

Shasta Gaughen, ed. *Contemporary Issues Companion: Endangered Species*. San Diego: Greenhaven Press, 2005.

Dale D. Goble, J. Michael Scott, Frank W. Davis,eds. *The Endangered Species Act at Thirty,* Vol. 1: *Renewing the Conservation Promise*. Washington DC: Island Press, 2005.

Dale D. Goble, J. Michael Scott, Frank W. Davis,eds. *The Endangered Species Act at Thirty,* Vol. 2: *Conserving Biodiversity in Human-Dominated Landscapes*. Washington DC: Island Press, 2005.

George C. McGavin, *Endangered: Wildlife on the Brink of Extinction*. Richmond Hill, Ontario: Firefly Books, 2006.

Ellis Richard, *The Empty Ocean*. Washington, DC: Shearwater, 2004.

Gene Wolfe, *Endangered Species*. New York: Orb Books, 2004.

Jennifer J. Yeh, *Endangered Species: Must They Disappear?* Information Plus, 2004.

Stephen M. Younger, *Endangered Species: How We Can Avoid Mass Destruction and Build a Lasting Peace*. New York: Ecco, 2007.

Periodicals

"Accelerating Loss of Ocean Species Threatens Human Well-Being," National Science Foundation, November 2, 2006.

"Animals on the Edge: Scientists Rush to Protect Earth's Rarest Species," *Junior Scholastic*, February 26, 2007, p6.

Doug Bandow, "Endangered Species Endanger Landowners' Rights," *Conservative Chronicle*, February 25, 2004.

Alan Burdick, "When Nature Assaults Itself," *New York Times*, April 22, 2003.

Chris Clarke, "No More Joshua Trees? Climate Change May Wipe Out the Signature Tree of the Mojave," *Earth Island Journal*, Spring 2007, p. 42.

Jamie Rappaport Clark, testimony before the U.S. Senate Subcommittee on Fisheries, Wildlife, and Water, Committee on the Environment and Public Works, Washington DC, May 19, 2005.

"Cloning Endangered Species—Watch Out!" Treehugger. com, May 25, 2005. http://www.treehugger.com/files/2005/05/cloning_endange_1.php

Nick Dusic, "Secure People Need Healthy Ecosystems," British Ecological Society, September 2005.

"Endangered Species: The Environmental Movement," *Economist*, February 18, 2006, p. 33.

Charlie Furniss, "Sea Change: The World's Commercial Fisheries Are in Terminal Decline," *Geographical*, February 2007, p. 48.

"Saving the Sea Cow: Can Manatees Stay Afloat?" *WR News*, Edition 4, September 15, 2006, p. 4.

Amy Hembree. "Cloning Is No Extinction Panacea," *Wired*, February 13, 2001, p. 2.

Derrick Z. Jackson, "Neglecting Mother Earth," *Liberal Opinion Week*, February 14, 2005.

Sarah James, "We Are the Ones Who Have Everything to Lose," *Wild Earth*, Winter 2003/2004.

Scott Kirkwood, "Too Much of a Good Thing? Elk Overpopulation in Rocky Mountain National Park Is Taking a Toll on the Ecosystem, and the Results Can't Be Ignored Any Longer," *National Parks*, Fall 2006, p. 8.

Janet Larsen, "Empty Skies," *USA Today*, March 2006, p. 51.

Jane Braxton Little, "Treasure Island," *Audubon*, September-October 2006, p. 74.

T. R. Mader, "Endangered Species Act: Flawed Law," Abundant Wildlife Society of North America, March 11, 2004. www.aws.vcn.com/flawed/html.

Brian Nowicki, "Delays in Endangered Species Act Protections Lead to Extinctions," *Earth Island Journal*, Autumn 2004.

Richard W. Pombo, "The ESA at 30: Time for Congress to Update and Strengthen the Law,"www.cdfe.org, 2005.

Susanne Quick, "Conservationists Debate Cloning Rare Species," *Milwaukee Journal Sentinel*, March 29, 2005.

Paul Raffaele, "Curse of the Devil's Dogs: Traditionally Viewed as Dangerous Pests, Africa's Wild Dogs Have Nearly Been Wiped Out. but Thanks to New Conservation Efforts, the Smart, Sociable Canines Appear Ready to Make a Comeback." *Smithsonian*, April 2007, p. 58.

Bret Schulte, "Is the Endangered Species Act in Danger?" *U.S. News & World Report*, April 23, 2007, pp. 40–41.

Mike Stark, "Will Logging Save the Spotted Owl?" *High Country News*, March 12, 2001 http://www.hcn.org/servlets/hcn.Article?article_id = 10301

Sylvia Pagan Westphal, "Copy and Save," *New Scientist*, June 19, 2004: 36–40.

"What Is It About Cuddly Animals That Overrides the Rational Faculty of Policymakers?" *National Review*, January 29, 2007.

Kurt Williamsen, "Destruction of the Oyster Industry: Though There Are an Estimated Five Billion Eastern Oysters in U.S. Waters, the National Marine Fisheries Service Is Considering Listing Them," *New American*, June 26, 2006, p. 31

WebSites

Endangered Species Coalition (www.stopextinction.org) The Endangered Species Coalition speaks on endangered species issues for some 360 environmental, conservation, religious, scientific, humane, sporting and business groups around the country. They use public education, scientific information and citizen participation to consider the fate of threatened and endangered species.

International Fund for Animal Welfare (www.ifaw.org). Engages communities, government leaders, and like-minded organizations around the world and achieve lasting solutions to pressing animal welfare and conservation challenges-solutions that benefit both animals and people.

National Library for the Environment (www.ncseonline. org). This site brings together information and resources on a large variety of environmental topics.

Rainforest Alliance (www.rainforest-alliance.org). This site offers face sheets and research papers about sustainable living and the preservation of biodiversity, as well as links to other conservation Web sites.

SeaWeb (www.seaweb.org). Offers ocean news and events, educational material, and links to ocean-related sites.

World Environmental Organization (www.world.org). Provides information on the environment, as well as numerous links to other environmental Web sites.

World Resources Institute (www.wri.org). Offers environmental news, educational material, links to environment-related sites, and global environment information.

Index

International Society
  of Tropical Foresters
  (ISTF), 116
International Trade Report,
  113
Internet, 104–105, 109
Introduction, 63, 88
Iowa, 99
Islands, 21
IUCN. *See* World
  Conservation Union

Jobs, 9–10, 24, 41–42,
  45, 74–76

Kansas, 99
Kenya, 17
King Pilly pine, 16

Lacey Act, 101
Laws, 39, 43, 101–103
Levitra, 59
Limbaugh, Rush, 76
Livestock, 43, 52
Lizards, 18–19
Logging, 7, 15, 41–42,
  74–76
Louisiana, 39, 47–48, 99
Louisiana State
  University, 48–49

Macaques, 56, 60
Madagascar, 15
Maine, 99

Mammals, 13–14, 16,
  20–21, 97–98, 101–102
Mariana Islands, 100
*Marine Mammal Protection
  Act,* 101
Maryland, 42, 99
Maryland Natural
  Heritage Program, 42
Massachusetts, 42, 99
Medicine, medicinal. *See
  also* Pharmaceuticals,
  21, 55–58, 73, 85
Megafaunas, 14–15
Mexico, 39
Michigan, 99
Migratory Bird Treaty
  Act, 101
Migratory patterns, 20
Minnesota, 99
Mississippi, 99
Modern Language
  Association (MLA), 68,
  108
Mollusks, 21, 97–98
Monkeys, 22, 84
Montana, 45, 99
Mountains, 14
Mussels, 9

National Library for the
  Environment, 122
National Marine
  Fisheries Service
  (NMFS), 39

Picture Credits

Cover: © Frank Lukasseck/zefa/Corbis

AP Images, 8, 11, 19, 20, 25, 26, 31, 36, 40, 44, 49, 52, 58, 60

About the Editor

Lauri S. Friedman earned her bachelor's degree in religion and political science from Vassar College in Poughkeepsie, NY. Her studies there focused on political Islam. Friedman has worked as a non-fiction writer, a newspaper journalist, and an editor for more than 7 years. She has accumulated extensive experience in both academic and professional settings.

Friedman has edited and authored numerous publications for Greenhaven Press on controversial social issues such as gay marriage, Islam, energy, discrimination, suicide bombers, and the war on terror. Much of the *Writing the Critical Essay* series has been under her direction or authorship. She was instrumental in the creation of the series, and played a critical role in its conception and development.